Finding *Love* at *Forty*

A Middle-Aged Quest for Happiness during a Global Pandemic

DOUGLAS JENNINGS

PAGE PUBLISHING
Conneaut Lake, PA

First originally published by Page Publishing 2024

ISBN 979-8-88960-919-3 (pbk)
ISBN 979-8-88960-950-6 (digital)

Printed in the United States of America

C O N T E N T S

Meet the Bachelor

To surrender dreams—this may be madness.

—Miguel de Cervantes

Life wasn't supposed to be this way. A middle-aged man-about-town, *Bumble*-ing and un-*Hinged*, going out barhopping, swiping left and right, booking dates every night of the week, mixing up my dates' names and hometowns, and all while my body slowly decaying from the inside as I lurch toward an age where mandatory cancer screenings are a way of life. Preposterous.

So how did I get here? I'm not entirely sure, but I'll recall to the best of my ability. I grew up in the Midwest, just outside Detroit, in a four-square-mile town called Fraser. I had a fairly normal childhood to the best of my recollection. I didn't date much in high school, as I was focused on earning a scholarship to pay for college. At least that's the version of the story that I like to tell myself. In reality, I had atrocious acne, braces, and zero game when it came to talking to girls—you know, typical male teenage angst.

I was a late bloomer when it came to dating, but I eventually came out of my shell once I got to college. The thing about dating in Michigan is that people do it with a purpose. And that purpose is to get married young. Most of my friends from high school did not enroll in a four-year university degree program, which means for these folks, marriage and starting a family was the next logical step right out of high school.

For those who did go to college, marriage by twenty was generally expected. If you were not married by twenty and you were not still in school, people would start to wonder. "Maybe he has wicked foot odor" and "I heard she's a biter" were just a few of the rumors floating around the warped little water cooler that was dating in small-town Middle America. Indeed, to avoid being presumed a leper for being unwed by twenty-two, one must attend graduate school, which is precisely what I did, choosing to pursue a career as a pharmacist.

While I like to poke pejoratively at this Midwestern marriage fixation, I actually have a deep respect for the institution. I was fortunate to grow up in a house with two loving parents who also had a (mostly) functional marriage. I'm not sure if that's where the foundation of my hopeless romanticism began, but I suppose it very likely had something to do with it.

Maybe I watched too many Disney movies growing up, but I've always believed that falling madly in love with the "the one" was my destiny. And despite my pursuit of science, order, reason, and desire to work in health care and healing the sick, I still had a very strong desire to get married and start a family. You could call these two pursuits—of medicine and love—as my tandem passions, my two great life quests.

Characterizing my relationship with the idea of marriage as "deep respect" is probably underselling things a bit. I would say that deep down inside, even as a young kid, I was borderline obsessed with it. I can remember being so young, still just growing up, and remembering that one of the first things I did when I saw someone new was to zone in their left ring finger. And when I saw it was empty (i.e., devoid of a ring), I immediately felt pity for that person. If it were a man whose hand I was inspecting, I would imagine him hunched over a tray table, eating a warmed-up TV dinner alone in a disorderly apartment while watching sports and drinking cheap beer. If it were a woman, I would imagine her also alone and lonely at home in an immaculate apartment, knitting a pair of socks for one of her ten cats.

I have no idea when these notions even started since they've been there for as long as I've made memories. And I still do this even today. Even with all the "work" I've done on myself, I still can't shake this subconscious little tick. Without fail, every time I meet a new person, or even see a stranger passing on the street, my eyes track immediately down their left arm to their ring finger.

So with that backdrop in mind, dear reader, it should not surprise you that love and marriage became a major focus of my life, even though I was still just in college. Indeed, I diligently dated my pharmacy school girlfriend all through grad school, and the only reason we did not wed the day after graduation like the rest of our classmates was because I left to pursue my postdoc training in Charleston, South Carolina.

The decision to leave was a hard one, for I knew in my heart that it would likely end the relationship. As much as I cared for her, I knew that I had to leave. My dual quests were at war with each other, and this time, science and healing won over true love. I knew that the training that I would receive would be foundational to everything that I would eventually want to become as a scientist and a scholar within the profession of pharmacy. And so I left in July of 2005, and after a brief long-distance affair, we separated after Thanksgiving of that same year.

Undeterred in my pursuit of both quests, I returned to Michigan after finishing my postdoc training to turn my attention back to finding true love. And within a year of returning, I met my future wife. She was a physician, and we met at the hospital were we both worked. Little did I know that this would be the last relationship that would start IRL—in real life. Every consequential relationship to follow this one would begin online.

I suppose that last sentence was a bit of an ominous foreshadow regarding the outcome of my first marriage. Like most relationships, life was grand for the first several years of our relationship. She eventually moved into my place, and after about a year of dating, we got engaged. In September of 2012, we got married down in her hometown of Miami. After we got hitched, we spent the next year back in Michigan while she finished her residency training.

However, once we relocated to her hometown in South Florida in 2013, things began to deteriorate. Unfortunately, I had taken a dead-end job in order to facilitate the move, and I was finding that my quest for greatness within my career was starting to suffer greatly. She worked a lot of strange hours as an emergency medicine physician; and in the long hours of silence in our sterile downtown Miami apartment alone, I started to worry endlessly that my career would end and I would never achieve the things I had set out to accomplish when I chose to be a pharmacist. In other words, my quests were at war again.

While we attempted to talk through these issues, we eventually just started to fight a lot. Her entire family was there, and she was not interested in relocating anywhere else, even temporarily. I knew in my heart that I could not stay there any longer without losing the very core of myself—that part that made me feel like me. As much as it gutted me, I had to leave. I knew if I stayed, I would eventually lose myself down there, and the relationship would likely end eventually anyway when she woke up one day and couldn't recognize the man that she had married anymore. In my head, I told myself that my sacrifice would save us both.

When I was at my darkest hour, fate intervened. I saw a random posting, not just for a job but *the* job. The heart transplant program at Columbia University Medical Center in New York was hiring for a full-time pharmacist. Not only was this exactly what I wanted to do, but it was also *the* place to do it. The Columbia team was world-renowned for their research in heart transplantation, and I knew immediately that I could achieve the greatness I was seeking as a scientist, scholar, and healer within their hallowed walls.

I applied, interviewed, and accepted the position the Monday after Thanksgiving in 2014. My wife and I separated in January of 2015.

My life in the Big Apple began rather unceremoniously. While my wife and I split amicably, a tax snafu had left us with no savings to divide up upon our separation. I hence moved into hospital housing with about $5,000 to my name. Like so many cliché New York City moving stories, I slept on the floor while awaiting my mattress delivery and used empty boxes as furniture for the first month or so. But despite these minor hardships, I was happy to be starting fresh in a new city.

But now what? Despite the divorce, my hopes for true love were not dashed. After years of having to sacrifice myself to preserve the marriage, moving to New York and prioritizing my needs actually reinvigorated me. Feeling like myself for the first time in a while, I found my zeal for my quest for true love slowly returning as the months ticked by post-divorce.

While I wanted to start dating again, I was at a loss for where to begin, not knowing anyone in the city. This was completely uncharted territory for me, given that I had always met people naturally through work or mutual friends. Finding my one true love in a city of eight million people seemed completely daunting, and I really didn't know how to begin. But the alternative was to end up a fifty-something spinster hanging out in bars and hitting on women twenty years younger than me—gross. No, I had to come up with something.

I had heard about online dating but was very leery to try it. The stories about daring apps in those days mostly revolved around Tinder and Grindr, and they seemed solely geared for hooking up. While I found the idea of anonymous sex to be mildly interesting, I figured that was probably easy to find that at a local bar. So in my initial months back into the dating environment in New York City, I tabled the idea of online dating and instead started hanging out at said local bars.

Then I bought a copy of the book *Modern Love* by the dating prophet and *Master of None* himself, Aziz Ansari. I actually found this book to be quite comforting in this critical juncture of my dating life. I can remember reading it while sitting outside Café Fiorello on the crisp fall weekends of 2015 after treating myself to brunch. I found the idea of modern dating to be very foreign and intimidating, and his book made me feel much less alone in those sentiments. In a way, it gave me the courage I needed to finally create a profile and put myself out there on the dating apps for the first time.

Armed with his sage wisdom of Prophet Ansari, I embarked on my quixotic quest for true love. Having grown up in a small town my whole life and just dating people that I ran into at work or through friends, I had never really needed a quixotic quest for romance before. Indeed, all my prior relationships had really just fallen into my lap. I would meet someone at work or school, ask them out, they said yes, and that was that. No apps, no chasing, no quest.

While the process of meeting people in my Midwestern life had come easily, I was about to find out that dating in the Big Apple was anything but. If only I knew a modicum of what was to come in terms of the toil, setback, confusion, bodily harm, and general mayhem that accompanied dating in New York City as a middle-aged man during a global pandemic, I would have started therapy much, much sooner.

But therein lies the very nature of questing. Google agrees, for when I asked it for the definition of a quest, it told me that a quest is a long or arduous search for something.

Arduous doesn't sound great, but I suppose that the best things in life are worth fighting for, right? I'll never forget the story of my mom when she used to tell me about her "Busha." Busha was their Polish word for grandmother, and every day, Busha would head to the market to get dinner. Back in those days, the whole family lived in one three-story house, with Busha up in the attic while the younger generations lived below.

So Busha had a lot of mouths to feed. And there were many Bushas who went to the market every day looking for dinner. In fact, so the story goes, there were more Bushas in search of chickens than chickens to be had. So every day, my mom's Busha had to fight the other Bushas for the chicken. How exactly this fight transpired is a mystery, for I never met my mom's Busha; and unfortunately, cell phone cameras didn't exist back then. Needless to say, my mom's Busha always fought for the chicken. And the family never went hungry (so the story goes).

So that's the lesson that I grew up with. My mom would always say, "Douglas, you have to fight for the chicken." Pondering this important life lesson as I was about to set out on my quest, I wondered what my future wife would think if she knew that I thought of her as a prize chicken.

The thing about quests is that they are more than just an arduous set of tasks. Google's definition goes on to say, "Quests often have a spiritual or moral component and may involve a search for knowledge, self-discovery, or enlightenment."

Was I prepared to face-plant on a few dates as I reentered the market? Yes, absolutely. Was I prepared to have to overcome the natural bodily shortcomings of being middle-aged at the beginning of this quest? Yes, I was. But enlightenment? Self-discovery? I'm a fully formed adult, after all, and a survivor of a divorce. I've made it to my midthirties and was ascending in my career, fresh off my move to the Big Apple. What else could there be to learn about myself at this stage?

Oh, how little did I know then how much I had to learn about the true nature of my quest and about how much self-discovery and enlightenment that I truly needed to experience to become the person that I already thought that I was. Nor could I have ever anticipated that a big goddammed global pandemic was going to erupt right in the middle of my wife hunting and send me down a path that I would have never anticipated back in those early days of 2016.

Well, I think that's enough about me, dear reader. Let's get to it now, shall we?

C H A P T E R   2

Waking up in Vegas

Get up and shake the glitter off your clothes, now!
That's what you get for waking up in Vegas!

—Katy Perry

My eyes opened and my body shuttered, jolted from sleep in a dark, unfamiliar room. My head was throbbing, and my body was feeling cold despite being under a heavy comforter. My mouth was dry, arid in fact. My senses were dulled to the point that it took me about thirty seconds to figure out where I was. The person snoring next to me was an effective hint that I wasn't alone, nor was I in my hotel room. *Ugh,* I thought to myself. *I feel like I've been drugged.* Later in the day, I would eventually remember that I was, in fact, drugged.

It was December of 2019, and I was in Vegas for a conference. These adventures to the desert of sin were a perennial occurrence, as one of the biggest pharmacy conferences is routinely held there. So while I was no stranger to Vegas, this year was a little different. For starters, I wasn't married for the first time in a while. And I was coming off a long year of failures in my quixotic quest for true love. Both of these variables had me in the mood to get into trouble at this conference.

8

My last serious relationship has ended in January of 2019. She was a wonderful person, a beguiling Canadian beauty with a heart of gold. Her name was Marie, and we had met at the 2017 version of this same conference in Orlando. We didn't start dating romantically until later in 2018; but when we did, we found that we vibed well together and matched energies on humor, politics, family orientation, etc. Despite the fact that we lived in different countries, we found a way to see each other quite often thanks to her travel as a pharmaceutical sales rep. Sadly, our love was star-crossed, as we had no means to eventually live in the same country. Winnipeg, as it turns out, is not so close to New York; and the distance eventually became too great to overcome. So being that the relationship would never lead to marriage and, hence, could never satisfy my quixotic quest for a wife and a life partner, I had to end it. I was very sad to do it at the time, but I knew that I needed to be true to my quest. And having a girlfriend in a faraway country was not part of the plan.

Unfortunately, the rest of 2019 was mostly a lot of dead-end dating on the apps. This disappointment was honestly unexpected, as during my first foray into online dating back in 2016 had been a one-and-done situation. The first person that I matched with on Bumble ended up being a long-term partner, so when I jumped back on the apps in 2019 after breaking up with Marie, I don't think that I was quite prepared for the amount of disappointment that was to follow.

These setbacks were making me start to hate online dating, which was a befuddling and onerous process. For my dear readers who haven't had the misfortune of ending up on one of these apps, let me elaborate a bit. For the first part of this strange process, one must create a profile. This is perhaps the most daunting part. At the heart of the conundrum is the enteral question of dating: Do I be myself, or do I send in my representative? Anyone who's dated before should know what I mean by "representative." If you're unfamiliar, he's a handy definition from ChatGPT:

In dating, the term "my representative" usually refers to the version of oneself that a person

presents to a potential partner during the early
phases of a relationship. This version of oneself
is often idealized and may not necessarily reflect
the person's true self.

So my first task was to figure out how honest to be. Ideally, the answer would be to be brutally honest, right? I mean, if the goal was to find a life partner, what good was it to embellish or, worse, to flat out lie? Unfortunately, the format for online dating profiles lends itself nicely toward embellishment, and given how many people were online dating in New York, I decided that I had to strike a balance between the brutal truth and a little bit of effective, um, selling.

First comes the pictures, which can often be the most agonizing part. Most apps limit to five or six pics, so any potential dater must be choosy about which to post. "Definitely start with a good shot of your face" was some critical advice that Prophet Ansari highlighted in his modern dating manifesto. So I selected a nice one of me in a suit—gaze averted left—which showed off my strong chin, one of my best features (so I'm told).

Should I have used a picture of me in a suit? Maybe not. But it was the best (and clearest) view of my face, which I thought over-ruled the fact that I looked a little square.

With that hurdle cleared, I set about to pick the remaining pho-tos. I was always careful to include one shot of my whole body, so my potential suitors could decide if my body type was what they're into. The height is the most important thing. I had learned from my time online dating that some women had minimum height requirements for their partners. Indeed, the first app that I downloaded back in 2016 was Tinder, and many girls around this time in New York had posted their minimum height preference in their profile.

The remainder of the pictures should generally showcase one's personality, so I chose various photos of me volunteering or traveling to fun places. Hopefully, this would convey to my dates that I was a well-rounded guy with diverse interests and an active social life. Now with my inchoate profile beginning to take shape, I was onto the next step: writing about myself.

Some apps like Hinge only ask for answers to prompted questions. Most are silly, like "Together we could." The "Two truths and a lie" was another popular prompt that was meant to break the ice. I actually preferred using this one. Mine were "Never been to India, broken the same bone three times, and used to pole vault in high school."

Many apps, however, like Bumble, did not have any prompts. You were simply presented with a blank canvas, on which you were to distill your entire worth as a life partner to a few hundred words. What an absolutely formidable proposition. How does one even begin to tackle this? I spent quite a bit of time pondering what to write here. My initial response reflected how I felt as a simple Midwestern guy in the big city.

"Just a normal guy. In all ways adequate, in no ways exceptional. Obviously since I'm on this app, I'm looking for love in all the wrong places."

While pithy, this lacked depth and didn't convey enough of what I was seeking in a partner. My second attempt was a bit more detailed: "Paunchy, middle-aged pharmacist seeking sturdy drinker partner for marriage. Must love cheese, poop jokes, and be willing to co-parent a quasi-feral cat."

Honest, yes. But perhaps a little too honest; and while this would resonate with my fellow Michiganders, I needed something more sophisticated for the New York City audience. I eventually settled on something that I think depicted both who I was and what I was looking for. While the version of this blog did evolve slightly over the years it was used, the core of it remained largely intact:

> Just a down-to-earth Midwestern guy. I love sports, reading, being outdoors, travel, creative writing, breweries/bourbon, the NYT, and road trips. Right now I'm working on learning Spanish and advancing my yoga practice. I'm hoping that you are looking for something serious and are ready to settle down and start a family.

Years later, after I was through therapy, I would add details regarding my attachment style, my enneagram, and my Myers-Briggs. After all, pop psych is all the rave these days. But in those early days, that was pretty much my sales pitch.

I know what you may be thinking. Seems pretty bland, right? Well, if you've ever been on a dating app in New York, you would understand how bland was in fact a distinguishing characteristic. The East Coast dating environment was one that I was completely unprepared for, and this geographic tension was quite palpable for me almost as soon as I entered the dating market.

For starters, many of my fellow daters on the apps in New York felt quite pretentious to me, and their inflated sense of achievement and accomplishment felt like steel wool rubbing abrasively against my simple middle-American sentiments. So many people's profiles read like social CVs rather than dating profiles, all freshly adorned with a list of the eighty-seven countries they'd traveled in the past year, the laundry list Broadway playbills they'd acquired over Christmas break, or the number of marathons they'd ran since last Tuesday.

Don't get me wrong. I'm into all these things. I love travel, theater, and fitness. But there's a way to portray this without seeming pretentious or self-inflating, and many of the profiles I was seeing seemed more intended on dazzling me with credentials versus actually showing me the real person behind the profile.

And then there was the scheduling. My god, was it infuriating. So many times I would match with someone, we'd have some nice dialogue on the app and then when I moved in to solidify a time to meet up, I'd get a response like this: Oh well, I'm going on Zimbabwe for a quick business trip this week. And then when I get back, I'm going to be working eighty hours a week for two weeks to hit this deadline. And then I have brunch with my besties for the following two weekends. So basically, I can meet up in four weeks on Tuesday. How does that sound?

I'm being intentionally hyperbolic in my caricature here, I realize that; but hopefully, you appreciate my point. After all, I was busy. Everyone in New York is busy. But the way many of these people on the apps portrayed themselves as "so busy" did not feel genuine and was yet another attempt at masquerading as this hyper-successful New Yorker.

Needless to say, I found this very, very frustrating, as it didn't feel like these individuals were truly serious about finding love.

I think that I should clarify my frustration by explaining that there are apps for casual dating, and I was not on those apps. My two consistent platforms were Hinge and Bumble, which were very relationship focused. Hinge's motto is "designed to be deleted." So running to slews of people who were on these relationship-focused apps but were "too busy" to meet up for a first date felt like running into a brick wall over and over.

I like dating successful, educated women. I'm actually a bit of sapiosexual, which shouldn't come as a surprise given that my first wife is a physician. There is actually an app called "The League," which on its face appears to be geared toward matching educated, successful people. Imagine that Tinder and LinkedIn had a child, and you would get The League.

After struggling with Hinge and Bumble, I thought I should at least try The League. After several months of waiting for admission in their queue, I was finally admitted. And yes, there's a wait for men to get in. This should have been enough of a red flag to not join, but at this point, I was desperate enough to try even this.

On this app, everyone had a C-suite title or had just started (and sold) their first company. To see someone not wearing a suit in their profile pic was an anomaly. Given that I had been rocking a suit pic in my other apps, I thought perhaps I was finally in the right place.

Oh, how wrong I was. Women in The League were even more elusive than in the other apps, and finding a mutually agreeable time to meet up was nearly impossible. My one and only date with someone I met on The League was with a former headmistress (that was her real title) of a prominent ballet company. On our second date, after she found out that I was a pharmacist, she tried to shake me down for Adderall so that she could learn the scores for the ballets more easily. Needless to say, there was not a third date, and my time on The League in 2019 was very short-lived.

These complaints aside, I think that the elephant in the room that we still need to discuss about online dating is one that transcends the profiles and the somewhat superficial approach that many New Yorkers take to dating. It's the idea of this entire process, which I had a hard time wrestling with going back to my nascent days dating online. This entire process of making a profile, posting pictures, and reducing your potential as a husband into two hundred words seemed profoundly antithetical to the entire spirit of finding love. Swiping right or left to choose a life partner? You have to be fucking kidding me.

As my quixotic quest ground onward through 2019, I quickly found myself realizing the banality of this entire practice of swiping left or right as a means to determine one's destiny. How was it that we as a society had de-evolved into this insta-judgment frame of mind, one where we so crudely distilled finding a life partner to the fickle flick of a finger? It had certainly started to feel like we had irrevocably warped the entire playing field of romance, and as that long year ground on, I eventually felt like I was trivializing the whole process of finding my forever partner.

It all felt so reductive. After all, finding a partner was supposed to be about love, about romance, and about establishing a true connection with another human being. Meeting a stranger in person, albeit a somewhat random and arbitrary way to find a mate, felt so much more organic than staring a picture of someone wearing four marathon medals and grinning vapidly through the small screen of my phone.

Online dating certainly has its advantages. As sage Ansari outlined in one of the opening chapters of his book, many marriage records from the early 1900s in New York showed that not only did people marry within their own neighborhood but many also actually married within their own building! Now with the apps, the whole of New York City—which is basically a microcosm of the entire world—is literally delivered to one's fingertips. So much diversity of choice can undoubtably be a good thing, as the apps can greatly expand the dating pool beyond one's immediate neighborhood.

Conversely, too much choice can also be a bad thing.

I am by no means a Casanova, but there were times where my inbox was overflowing with matches. And I must admit that over time, I found that this reduced the value that I placed on each individual person who matched with me. These people had taken the time to go through the same agonizing introspection that I had gone through to design a fetching profile. And yet as the number of matches just kept coming and kept accumulating, I found myself subconsciously starting to change under the weight of all of this choice.

After all, why would I spend time trying to get to chatting extensively online with one person whom I just matched with when I have ten other matches waiting to chat? And if I did make it out on a date with someone, I knew in the back of my mind that if things don't go well that I have so many other choices that I could just move on without exploring the connection further. Indeed, it was a very pernicious process that was taking hold of me in 2019, one that was slowly eroding my sense of patience and respect for other daters. It was late in the fall of that year that I finally realized that this insidious erosion in my core dating values was occurring.

The problem was that I was so obsessed with my quixotic quest that I found it very hard to disengage from the apps, even if only temporarily. I was type A in all facets of my life, and since moving to New York, I was especially type A in my approach to my quest. There was to be no rest until I had prevailed in finding my person, even if the process of finding her was slowly dehumanizing and demoralizing me.

Cue Las Vegas. This trip caught me at just the right time. I mean, if there was one city that I could go where the pressure to find a life partner would disappear, it was Vegas. It was a sort of forced vacation from dating, a geographic barrier to push me off the apps for a week and recharge my depleted love batteries. So when I booked my flight in mid-November, I felt a sense of relief—like the vacation that I desperately needed was about to arrive. I even booked a room at the Cosmo on the off chance that I was lucky enough to find a willing partner in crime for the week of debauchery.

When the trip eventually came and I did get to my room in the Cosmo, I knew that I had made the right choice. The seductive artwork featured many beautiful, elegant women in various stages of getting ready for an evening out on the town. The dim lighting cast a warm, intimate glow throughout the space. The curtains were thick and luxurious, offering essential privacy from the outside world while creating an air of mystery and intrigue within. Even with all the contemporary decor, the bathroom was the lynch pin. The large walk-in rain shower dominated the space and was encapsulated on three sides with see-through glass walls.

Yep, the room was built for sex. I actually felt like the room would judge me if I didn't have sex in it. Under the weight of this pseudo peer pressure, I relented, and I made up my mind that I wouldn't let my hotel room down on this trip.

The conference itself was fairly boring and predictably prosaic, as most pharmacy conferences tend to be. The highlight of this particular conference was always the Sunday afternoon, which was usually when my friends and I would play hooky from the meeting and watch football all day. This tradition continued in 2019, when we all met at the sportsbook at the Mandalay Bay to grab a table, drink, and bet on the games. I was slightly delayed in arriving, and so the 1:00 p.m. games were already about half over when I found my friends huddled around a table near the back of the bar. When I finally approached the table, I saw that Andy was sitting with them.

Pharmacy is a small world, and I had known of Andy through the mutual professional waters that we both navigated, but I'd never met her in person before. As the group at the table was quite large and I had several friends that I needed to catch up with, I didn't talk to Andy at first. But by the second round of drinks, I found myself sitting across from her.

It was only after we started talking that I noticed how pretty she was. She had very luminescent green-blue eyes, a soft face, and a wry, disarming smile. Her sandy-brown hair landed about shoulder length, and when she pushed it back behind her ears, she revealed pearl earrings with a matching necklace. There was something timeless and classic about this choice in jewelry, something that immediately felt like home and connected me to her. She felt safe, like a safe and inviting presence, almost like a harbor for a vessel like mine, one that had been tossed and thrashed about for a year in the turbulent waters of hoity-toity East Coast dating.

Physically, she was athletic but not svelte. She was actually a little burly in the way that CrossFit people can be, which I later confirmed was one of her preferred workouts. As we talked, I soon found out how funny and down-to-earth she was. She was actually very easy to talk to, and we quickly killed a few hours chatting superficially about football and craft beers.

Unfortunately, we both had work dinners to attend, so around 4:00 p.m. or 5:00 p.m., we had to go our separate ways. I could definitely sense that we were both vibing on each other, so I put my number in her phone as I sped away to change back from my Lions jersey into my business attire.

My dinner was work related, of course. One of my colleagues had scored a new job working for a fledgling pharmaceutical company, and he wanted me in the audience of this program as moral support. While I was mildly interested in the topic and I did my best to pay attention, it was hard for me to not incessantly check my phone to see if Andy was texting. As the evening wore on, I started to regret giving her my number and not asking for hers in return. By ceding control of this evening to her, I started to feel as if I had squandered my golden opportunity to have the unattached sex that I so desperately needed at that point in my forlorn dating life. I had no idea how I was going to explain this failure to my hotel room.

Eventually, the dinner was winding down; and although my blood alcohol levels were up, my spirits were down. Other friends were filling my text inbox with invitations to hit one of Vegas's posh nightclubs, but no message had appeared from the alluring Andy. Dejected and downtrodden, I disembarked from the dinner and drudged back to my hotel room to face the music.

Upon entering my room, I could sense the judgment. I felt like all the eyes of the various women in the wall art were looking down at my sad, sexless self. I quickly scurried into the bathroom to take a cold shower, only to be reminded about the sexy shower setup, which, even though it lacked eyes, was also judging me.

After an unsatisfying solo shower in the super-sexy glass box, I unpacked my nighttime accessories and started preparing for bed. In addition to the usual items—toothbrush, facewash, floss, etc.—I had packed an impressive array of sleeping meds.

I had always had trouble sleeping, going back to when I was young. I can remember being twelve years old and being completely unable to fall asleep. I used to listen to music to help distract my brain, which was too busy even back at that tender prepubescent age. I can remember having to get up three to four times to flip the cassette as I lay in bed, making steady eye contact with the ceiling of my parent's basement. For those readers who are too young to remember cassettes, they held about twenty to thirty minutes of music per side. So yeah, I was lying awake awhile.

As I had aged, my insomnia had steadily worsened; and by the time I was in my late thirties and at this particular Vegas conference, I had constructed an impressive pharmacologic armamentarium. The fact that I had been drinking all night did not abate my insomnia one bit, and so I lined up my meds one by one as I mindlessly brushed my teeth. My usual go-to sleeping med was actually not a sleeping med at all. It was Benadryl. For you see, my dear reader, I'm actually quite allergic to my roommate—the hirsute quadruped who inhabits my apartment, pays no rent, and judges me relentlessly for all my dating foibles. Thank god the cat's English skills are still rudimentary, for if she were to write this book, it would have a much more scathing undertone than the flattering version that I'm presenting.

Benadryl happens to cause profound sedation as a side effect, which is usually unwanted unless one happens to be an insomniac. So down the hatch went the little pink pill. And for my side dish, I had packed some melatonin to help with the jet lag. Down went ten milligrams of that.

It was nearly 1:00 a.m. when I climbed into bed, and having finished tranquilizing myself, I was scrolling aimlessly on Instagram, waiting for the drugs to kick in. It was then that fortune swung my way.

"Hey, I'm so sorry. I just finally escaped from this endless drug dinner! Did you want to still get a drink?"

This text appeared on my phone screen like a bat signal. I immediately shot up in bed and inspected the number, which came from an unknown sender.

"Hey, is this Andy?" I daftly replied.

"Of course, it is, dude. LOL. How many women are you expecting to hear from tonight?"

Her reply was pointed and funny. If she only knew that I was presently in my hotel room with skin cream on my face and a belly full of Benadryl to contain my unwieldly allergies to my feline child. And no, in case you're wondering, the fact that the cat was 2,500 miles away did not matter, for her hair was wedged into every crevice of every item that I possessed; and I would have needed to run myself and my luggage through a carwash to clean myself to the point of not needing the Benadryl.

With the bat signal hence flashed, what was our hero to do? Do I text back that I'm a late-thirties insomniac and I've already drugged myself for the night, and hence, I'm sorry, Andy, that your late-night booty call will go unfulfilled?

Of course not. I promptly shot out of bed, went into the bathroom, and shoved three fingers into my throat until I had emptied the contents of my stomach into the toilet.

Through the retching and tears streaming down my face, I thought that I could see a pink streak in my vomit. My blood alcohol level was not zero, so I was having a hard time discerning if that pink streak was the Benadryl or if it was blood from starching my throat with my fingers.

No matter. I didn't have any time left to ponder the contents of the toilet. I had told Andy that I would meet her in one of the bars in the Luxor where she was staying. I quickly cleaned up my face, brushed my teeth seven times, took a shot of mouthwash (I actually think I swallowed it, but I can't remember), and bolted out the door on toward my date with destiny.

After a nauseating cab ride, I managed to get to the Luxor and find Andy at the bar. She was sitting over in the corner at a small table in a dimly lit corner by herself. When I saw her, my heart skipped a beat. As the anticipation that had built all day was on the precipice of bursting, I sped over to her table.

She was even more beautiful now than I recalled from the afternoon. She was wearing fresh makeup (and the pearls still) and a very formfitting and flattering black dress. It was just short enough to show off her muscular legs, which were bursting with a kind of feminine strength that cut right through what tattered defenses I might have still had at that point. At this point, it was all systems go. I was not going to bed without Andy that night.

She asked me what I wanted to drink, and the best option sounded like an espresso martini. I felt that this would be the safest option, as hopefully, the caffeine would blunt some of the lingering sedatives still coursing through my bloodstream.

All was going well as we enjoyed our first round of drinks together. She and I had locked eye contact since I sat down and hadn't broken it during our flirtatious small talk, and I could feel her foot traveling up and down my calf under the table. We were well on the way to taking the party upstairs, when one of her colleagues from another company suddenly (and drunkenly) approached our table and started chatting with Andy.

I played polite and let them talk while I buried myself in my phone. Unfortunately, it was about now that I started to feel drowsy. I was just getting to the end of my espresso martini, and I suddenly felt the strength being sapped from my body. *Goddamn it*, I thought to myself. The sedatives were starting to kick in.

I mean, what did I really expect? My method of expunging these meds from my body was far from scientific. Feeling panicked, I excused myself from the conversation and ran to the bar. I ordered a shot of espresso and a diet coke, and I downed them both in about five minutes. I next ordered a soda water with lime to feign the appearance that I was drinking while Andy was carrying on with her colleague. My injection of caffeine was not really working, and I was actively on the struggle bus and doing by best to avoid passing out in the bar.

Finally, my window appeared, and another pharma guy came up and distracted Andy's colleague. I quickly approached her from behind and whispered into her ear, "If you want me, you have to take me home now."

At least that's what I hope I said. At this point, I was a walking pharmacy, and I might have just whispered actual gibberish into her ear. If any of you have seen the *Wolf of Wall Street* and you know the scene where Leo thinks his drive home on quaaludes was perfect—only to find out the next morning that it was far from—that's probably about how smoothly I was hitting on Andy at that point.

Regardless of what nonsense I slurred into her ear, she whirled around and, without hesitation, pulled me in by my belt and kissed me. It was quick, as we were still out in public, but it was enough to let me know that she had understood the message even if it was a little incoherent. I started walking toward the exit with my soda water, and she squared up the tab and followed behind so as not to raise too much suspicion. We found each other near the elevators, and as we waited alone, we slowly intertwined our fingers together.

As soon as we entered her room, my drunk and drugged brain was fascinated by the curved walls of the pyramid. I walked over in a stupor and started staring at the angles of the windows like an inebriated architect. I barely heard Andy latch the door, and when I turned around, she was marching toward me while peeling off and discarding her dress on the floor.

Epilogue

Throughout this book, I'll take the opportunity to do a little postmortem on each date and dissect out any lessons learned for you, the reader, to consider. In our first epilogue, I suppose I should first round out the rest of the story with Andy.

I did indeed black out the rest of the evening thanks to the impressive cocktail of alcohol and drugs in my system, but from what Andy told me the next morning, things went very well despite me not having a functioning human brain in my skull. Andy and I actually spent the whole next morning in bed chatting, and I really enjoyed getting to know her better when I was in a state of mind that was able to form new memories. Because pharmacy is a really small world, I can't disclose exactly where Andy is from, as that would be enough for people who know us both to figure out who she is. And yes, reader, if you haven't figured out that I'm using fake names for the women in this book, I guess now's the time to divulge that fact.

Andy was living in the South back in 2019, and she was divorced herself with a young son. She told me the whole story of their marriage, how it ended, and how she ended up moving over to Big Pharma to be able to spend more time with him (even though she only had shared custody). We definitely bonded over our respective divorces, and she opened my eyes to the difficulties of being a single mom. I sympathized with her struggles for how to still set a good family example to him in the postdivorce era, and I could very much empathize with the loneliness that she suffered on the weekends that he was with his father. Many of my weekends in New York in 2019 had been lonely ones. Were it not for the cat, I would have been at home watching rom-coms on Friday nights by myself. While her English skills are marginal at best, she's still good company.

But despite all the serious talk, we actually had a great time chatting. Andy was down-to-earth and funny. She had a great perspective on life, and although she was successful in her career, she was very family oriented. I liked all these things that I was seeing, so much so that I changed my flight to stay an extra night so that Andy and I could spend more time together. I actually went back to my super-sexy hotel room, blew a kiss to all the girls in the paintings on the walls, and packed up my stuff and moved to Andy's very prosaic, nonjudgmental hotel room. Honestly, I did feel a little like a conquering general marching back into that hotel room in the Cosmo. It was nice to get the last laugh there.

Andy and I had a nice dinner together on our last night in Vegas before flying out to our respective cities the next day. And while I did return to New York with Andy's glow on me and I actually considered inviting Andy to New York for a weekend, I quickly changed my mind after a few days. At this point, I was very much scarred from my year with Marie; and I had no will or energy to enter into another long-distance relationship, especially when factoring in that she had a young son. I have a soft spot for single mothers. I think that they are to be cherished and supported for their braveness in reentering the dating world. A man must never trifle with a single mother with respect to dating, for they don't have time or energy to waste on someone who's not all in. And unfortunately, because of the distance, I knew that I couldn't be all in with Andy.

This was a hard decision for me because Andy was a great person, and we connected so well in the limited time that we had together. But looking back now, I am proud of that younger version of myself who stuck to his guns. I think that a less mature younger version of me, oh, let's say, circa 2017, would have been blinded by Andy's charms and jumped into a doomed relationship, even though he knew in his heart that he didn't have the fortitude to see it through.

So if there is a lesson to be learned from this trip to Vegas, it's to thine own self be true. Even though Andy was alluring, I knew that it wouldn't work with the distance, and so I stayed true to my quixotic quest. Dating Andy would have only pulled me off course for a few months until the distance had become too inconvenient, at which time I would have had to end it anyway.

So in summary, my word for Andy is "reassurance." After spending the weekend with her, I felt reassured in my faith in my quest, mostly by resisting my more basic urges while still keeping my main objective in focus. But it easily could have also been "amazing." Andy was an amazing person that I happened to meet on a trip when I was looking for anything but. Were the physical circumstances of our respective locations more favorable, we may have ended up dating and finding out if we were meant to be.

But no matter, for once I was back in New York, I felt refreshed and freed from many of the doldrums that I had accumulated over the long 2019. I was really looking forward to 2020—a new year and a new decade—to finally kick off a reboot of my love life. I had even planned a *Great Gatsby*-themed New Year's Eve party in my apartment to usher in this new golden era of my life. I mean, certainly, if there were any bumps to present themselves in 2020, they would be minor and very easy to navigate. Certainly, nothing major could happen in 2020 to derail my renaissance not after the abysmal 2019 that I had had. Certainly not, right?

A Pandemic Birthday

Destiny guides our fortunes more favorably
than we could have expected.

—Miguel de Cervantes

In the quest for love in the Big Apple, sometimes life gets in the way. Usually, this takes the form of matching with a great catch on Bumble or Hinge right before one person goes away on a big trip. The pace of dating being what it is in New York, by the time the trip is over, one or both parties have inevitably moved on to other matches. In the instance of my thirty-ninth birthday, life got in the way with something much, much bigger.

It has barely been six months since Andy and I had our dalliance in Vegas, and I can scarcely recognize the world around me. Everything, and I mean almost everything, that I had my hopes tied to in the start of 2020 had been destroyed by the COVID-19 pandemic. With everything in a state of upheaval and spiraling toward my thirty-ninth birthday, my one possible savior from this misery ended up being a girl named Amy. And while Amy and I did not find true love in the midst of the largest global pandemic since the 1918 Spanish flu, we did provide each other a modicum of relief from what was a very, very trying time. Finding true love is always my primary dating goal; however, sometimes it's okay to aim smaller. In the case of my thirty-ninth birthday, I just needed to be rescued.

When it first started, the pandemic was an all-hands-on-deck emergency for all health-care providers. I didn't have time to think or to really feel anything because unless we were sick, we were all expected to pitch in and help. I was a transplant pharmacist, but all transplants ceased once the pandemic was full-blown. I was repurposed as a critical care pharmacist, and I was covering a makeshift intensive care unit that had been created in one of our operating rooms. Every day, I had to chart review twelve or so souls who were slowly dying on antiquated ventilators that would have never been suitable for use in modern medicine. We had no real treatments for COVID-19 back then, so every day, I basically signed into our electronic health record remotely from my kitchen table and then proceeded to watch these poor souls lurch toward their untimely demise.

But by the time my birthday was rolling around in June, the hospitals had all decanted, and work had slowed down to the point that things were no longer operating in emergency mode. On this dreary Friday, I was working from home, as the hospital still did not want too many of us congregating in one spot and spreading an infection that would take out half of the workforce at once.

The pandemic had introduced a degree of monotony, the likes of which I had never experienced. As nearly all social interactions carried the risk of catching a potentially lethal virus, my social circle had dwindled down to the semi-feral cat who shared my apartment. On my birthday, I awoke before my alarm, something that I had become accustomed to, as sleep was proving to be even more elusive than normal as the isolation dragged on. After doing some stretches, I tracked down the long hallway toward the kitchen that morning, still foggy from slumber. My senses were assailed as the cat bleated out ravenous complaints over her nocturnal famine, which I had long since become accustomed to as I robotically tossed a cup of meat pellets into her empty bowl.

Soon, the apartment filled with the scent of fresh coffee, and I assumed my position at my "work-from-home" station. My office living room was flanked by two large windows, which offered visage of a thick blanket of frumpy gray clouds. A steady drizzle fell, and cool strips of rain adorned the panes like blinds. A cold, sleepy city glowered back at me through the windows as my gaze drifted downward toward my monitor, which will occupy my attention for the next several hours.

COVID had changed so much of our physical word, and I had certainly not been spared. A neatly trimmed clean cut had given way to long strands of hair, which required a comb-over to avoid obstructing vision, and a woolly beard now coated my previously youthful face. Honestly, in hindsight, I'm not sure why it took me so long to grow that beard. Looking back now at pictures prior to the pandemic, I looked like a teenager without facial hair. I think of all things to come out of living through a pandemic, the beard is definitely a favorite of mine.

It is my thirty-ninth birthday, and the only silver lining that I can muster to cheer myself up is to mutter to the cat, "Thank god it's not my fortieth." The idea of missing a milestone birthday in isolation was something that I could not fathom, so I was glad at least to have missed it by one year. And while the cat is certainly fine company most nights, her English proficiency was still a bit lacking at the time, so I was finding the loneliness getting harder and harder to fend off. Indeed, I was quite envious of my friends, all of whom were either married or living with partners. I'm sure that they were doing more interesting things in quarantine than trying to teach a feline her ABCs.

Any prospects of a normal birthday that were not eliminated by pandemic restrictions were obliterated by the other major catastrophe that rocked society in 2020. For you see, my birthday is on the June 5, and two weeks prior, on the May 25, George Floyd was brutally murdered. While the subsequent movement for social justice that ensued was transformative for our collective psyche as Americans, the unfortunate social unrest was also transformative for the city. What few restaurants and establishments that hadn't been shuttered by the pandemic were now completely boarded up to deter looters, and the city was under a strict 8:00 p.m. curfew for all nonessential personnel.

The fact that it was raining on this dismal Friday afternoon was just icing on the cake, as hanging out in the park was virtually the only activity left available. I contemplated my options for what I could possibly do to celebrate after I had completed my work-from-home activities. Most of my friends also worked in health care, and many were either stuck in the hospital or too afraid to leave their apartments given the state of unrest in the city. Just when it seemed that I was destined to dine with the cat for my thirty-ninth birthday, fate interceded.

The week prior, just before the social unrest gripped the city, I went on a first date with a girl I met on Hinge. Amy and I had enjoyed a typical pandemic first date, one that involved walking and drinking. We met at Tacuba on Ninth Avenue in Midtown and ordered two extremely boozy Cadillac margaritas to-go. As we proceeded to drink our way through Hell's Kitchen, it became apparent that we had a lot in common. Amy was "age appropriate" as my sister would say, meaning that she wasn't a twenty-six-year-old still trying to find herself in the great big world of New York City's late-night party scene. She stood about 5'2", with big blue eyes and a very disarming laugh. She smiled with all her teeth, and by the time we had a second drink, she was holding my hand tightly.

Despite the strangeness of pacing around the neighborhood and publicly drinking in broad daylight, we had a great time. There was a lot of laughter and a lot of stories. I wish that I could share more details about our conversation, but sadly, the amnestic effects of the Cadillac margarita are quite potent. I can recall that after three drinks, we sealed the date with a nice kiss and parted ways to stumble back to our respective apartments.

In the upheaval that had followed the death of George Floyd, I had not had a chance to follow up with Amy since our first date. Then as I sat at my kitchen table on my birthday, preparing a dinner menu for the cat and I, Amy texted.

"WYD. LOL."

"Planning a six-course birthday feast for me and my cat. LOL. WYD?"

"Nothing. My work is basically shut down RN. Want to get drunk in the park?"

That text message was like Lazarus, and suddenly, my birthday plans were resurrected from the dead. I excitedly texted back that I indeed wanted to get hammered in the park, and we arranged to meet in an hour at a nearby Joe and the Juice. I giddily skipped back down the long hallway to my bedroom to start getting ready. Fortunately, the rain had tapered off to a steady mist; and despite the dampness, the temperature outside was actually quite warm. I picked out my favorite shirt, a coral-blue short-sleeved linen button down, and some bright-red shorts. The punch of color felt especially necessary for this droopy day. And then a fateful decision: I choose to wear my brand-new Cole Haan boat shoes. What could go wrong? After all, they're just boat shoes, right? What could be more comfortable than boat shoes?

There was one more item for me to take care of before departing. The pesky issue of the curfew. I was very excited to see Amy again, and I was not going to let this curfew stand in the way of this date. Not only was this date a life raft to save me from my loneliness, but it also carried the same promise that all dates do: true love and finding my forever person. If the date were going well and Amy and I were on our way to falling madly in love with each other, I absolutely did not intend to have evening truncated by this damn curfew. After a few minutes of pondering, I devised a cleaver solution. I grabbed a duffle bag and packed up my bat suit.

If you're wondering at this point, *Is this guy really going to risk getting arrested for breaking mandatory curfew for a second date with a girl that he just met on Hinge?* The answer is a resounding abso-fuck-ing-lutely yes.

With my plan in place, I grabbed a small hand cooler and filled it with hard seltzers and set off to meet Amy. We met outside the designated spot, and Amy was right on time. Donned with a white crop top and a pink floral skirt, she stood out from the drabness of the city like a Monet painting against a concrete wall. She greeted me with one of her ear-to-ear smiles, kissed my check, and whispered, "Happy birthday," into my ear. Her warmth washed over me like the morning sun, and I felt all the distress from the last week's chaos melting away.

Little did I know that when Amy suggested that we meet at the Joe and the Juice, it was to obtain mixers for our drinks. What I have failed to mention about Amy is that she worked for one of the major bourbon manufactures, and so she was very well-versed in all things liquor. Amy had brought an impressive selection of whiskey, tequila, and vodka to mix with our juice. To say that I was impressed with this spread is an understatement; as a sturdy drinker myself, Amy was clearly a woman after my own heart. She had indeed brought so much booze with her that she needed a small roller cart in order to tote everything along.

With our mixers in hand, we walked the few remaining blocks to Central Park. Few people were out, either driven away by the weather, the pandemic, or the social unrest. Our cart full of booze in tow, we strolled through the park until we found the Sheep's Meadow. As it was still misting, we sought shelter under a large tree at the north end of the meadow and spread out a blanket to have our picnic.

The scene was like something out of *The Twilight Zone*. It was the middle of a Friday afternoon, and Central Park was completely deserted. Not one other person sat with us on the entire Sheep's Meadow, which is astonishing given that this is one of the most popular areas in the park. The clouds and mist had erased all color, other than the green grass and the hues of our wardrobe. We sat silently under the tree at first, I think both shell-shocked at the surrealness of our surroundings. I looked over at Amy; the mist was settling on her face as little beads of water, and her big blue eyes shone like sapphires. She smiled brightly and asked, "What cocktail can I make for the birthday boy?"

As we imbibed in the rain, the conversation slowly picked up. Holding hands, we shared stories of our childhoods, moving to New York, and our favorite places to travel. As a means of escapism at its finest, we fantasized about where we'd go when all this was over. We had both spent a considerable amount of time in Western Europe, and we both loved the same things about the same cities. After a robust discussion of various options, we both settled on Paris as the preferred post-pandemic destination.

Amy also started to open up as the conversation went on. She, too, was on a quest for true love, and she dreamed one of settling down and buying an apartment with her future partner. She was dreadfully tired of renting and "making other people rich," as she put it. While I shared her sentiment, I had no desire to buy. Despite having lived in New York for over five years at that time, I always had this lingering sense that my time here was temporary and that sensation of being in limbo had prevented me from every really contemplating buying. What was creating that sense of disconnect from being able to settle down was my inability to find a partner, as I kept telling myself every year that if I didn't find someone to marry in all the craziness of New York that I would eventually have to move back to the Midwest and marry a farmer's daughter.

Amy, on the other hand, was very gung ho on purchasing, except that she was also waiting to find a partner before buying. In that moment, I felt a little sad that her dream was also deferred by the shitty New York dating scene. She and I both seemed stuck, unable to move forward on our own, our futures tied to capricious whims of Bumble and Hinge.

Reflecting on that sentiment now, I know that feeling of limbo was a toxic manifestation of my quixotic quest. Like Amy, I was waiting for my own "white knight" to rush in a save me and for us to ride off into the sunset and build a home together. Back then, I couldn't put words to what I was feeling, but armed with my current psychiatric vocabulary, I can say that I was devaluing my single existence as one unworthy of buying property alone. I was an incomplete person, and until I found my other half, I needed to maintain the degree of flexibility afforded to someone renting. By remaining in this transitory state, I could bend my world to fit my new partners and mold myself to them like a piece of freshly heated steel.

Obviously, there are lots of things wrong with this way of thinking. In hindsight, I clearly should have invested in myself and become the person that I wanted to be rather than remaining undefined so someone else could come along and define me. Now I can see how tragic my thinking was back then. But back then, I just felt lost, and I didn't really know why.

Anyway, back to the story. As our blood alcohol levels rose and the sunlight started dwindling, Amy leaned in and kissed me. I was slightly caught off guard, but I very quickly sank forward into her body and pressed my lips firmly against hers. That kiss was life-affirming, a burst of humanity against the backdrop of a city in mourning. It's a moment that I don't think I'll ever forget.

"Do you want to come back to my place? I have a full bar haha," she whispered archly.

"I don't think anything would make me happier."

We quickly packed up our soggy blanket and what remained of our mixers and headed out for Amy's apartment. As we left the park, I started to notice my feet weren't doing so well. As it would seem, my new Cole Haan boat shoes were indeed not only uncomfortable, but they were grating my feet like a block of parmesan cheese. Mercifully, Amy's apartment was only a few blocks from the park.

Upon entering Amy's place, I immediately liberated my feet from the satanic shoes, only to discover that they were covered in blisters. As distressing as this was, I thought to myself that this was a problem for later and turned my attention back to Amy. Her apartment was beautiful: large, spacious, and impeccably decorated. As advertised, she had a very full bar. There was even a popcorn machine in the corner.

"Do you like mescal?" she asked.

"Yeah, I love mescal. Tequila is a bit overrated in my opinion."

Thinking that my answer would earn me a mescal margarita or something similar, I plopped onto the sofa and sank into the cushion. Amy's apartment was warm and inviting, and I felt very at ease. I noticed a large book on the table titled *Whiskeys of the World*. Immediately intrigued, I began flipping through its pages, only to be quickly interrupted by Amy's first drink.

"Here you go," she said spritely as she handed me a vat of mescal with a few ice cubes floating along the rim of the glass.

"Good god," I exclaimed in surprise. "Is this the direction the evening is going to go?"

She quipped back wryly, "We'll see."

We popped some popcorn and settled onto the couch; our legs intertwined as we sipped our homewrecker cocktails. As the mescal disengaged my frontal cortex, my inhibitions vanished. Amy was quite a charmer if I do say so. She was very well-versed in bourbon and whiskey, sports (a die-hard Mets fan, but I forgave her for it), and books. We bonded over our shared affection for Matthew McConaughey and spent time swapping quotes and pop gossip stories that we'd heard about his involvement at Wild Turkey. And of course, we swapped our most disastrous New York City dating stories.

Suddenly, Amy shouted, "I don't have a cake for you on your birthday!"

"Why are you shouting?" I said with a chuckle as I attempted to regain my bearings from being startled by her sudden announcement.

She did not answer my question and instead shot up from the sofa and marched into the kitchen. Having received no instructions, it was unclear if I should follow her. Suddenly, the apartment fell dark as she drunkenly mashed her hand against the switch panel and turned off all the lights. She then emerged from the kitchen with three lit candles buried in a bowel of cough drops. She started stammering "happy birthday" as she slowly walked toward me with my "cake."

After I blew out my candles, she winked and whispered, "What did you wish for?"

"Nothing that I don't already have tonight," I said as I snapped a wink back.

We stared into each other's eyes briefly before I reached out and pulled her in close. She dropped the bowl, and cough drops scattered everywhere. We scarcely noticed as we started making out, and Amy guided my hands up her back to unsnap her bra. As we slowly descended to the couch, Amy grabbed my shoulders and pinned me down.

After a while of passionate kissing, we eventually settled down on the couch next to each other. I put my arms around her and pressed her face into my chest, and we sat silently, listening to each other's breathing as the soft glow from an unexpectedly full moon lit up the apartment. *A full moon on this of all birthdays*, I thought to myself. How fitting. Little did I know how important that full moon would be to my journey home.

It was the darkness outside juxtaposed to this bright moon that alerted me to the lateness of the evening.

"Oh shit, it's getting late. I should head back," I said sleepily. The mescal had certainly taken a toll at that point.

"But how are you going to get home?" she inquired. "It's way past curfew, and there are cops at checkpoints on every street. Do you just want to crash here tonight on the couch?"

"Don't worry," I replied. "I have a plan."

As I stood from the couch, my foot landed squarely on one of the cough drops, and it pressed deeply into one of the freshly made blisters. Before I can contain it, a shriek of pain escaped my lips. I quickly bit my tongue as I tried to wipe away the tears that were streaming down my face.

Amy whipped around in surprise and said, "What the hell was that? Are you okay?"

"Yes, yes, all good," I hissed quietly through clenched teeth as the pain shot up my leg and into my right butt cheek.

After I recovered from the damage inflicted by this tiny assailant, I began to execute my escape plan. It was time for the bat suit. I grabbed my duffle bag and whipped out my scrubs. As essential workers were exempt from the curfew as long as they were traveling to or from work, my plan was to masquerade as a more responsible version of myself returning from a shift. The plan was fail proof, as one of the hospitals that I worked with was in the same neighborhood as mine and Amy's apartment. Even the heavy stench of mescal on my breath could be somewhat camouflaged by the mandatory masking brought on by the pandemic.

My costume was perfect; I had even remembered my name badge. Armed with the courage that only comes with massive quantities of mescal, I was confident that I could BS my way past any NYPD checkpoint on the way home. Amy and I briefly kissed goodbye, and I thanked her profusely for an amazing birthday. Unfortunately, as I exited the lobby of her building, the literal Achilles heel of my plan was manifesting: the goddamned boat shoes.

I tried to walk several blocks toward my apartment, but it soon became evident that I was not going to make it. My feet actually started bleeding into the shoes, and I was limping so badly that I knew I would not make it through the checkpoint. Quickly, my alcohol-soaked brain tried to formulate a solution. There were no cabs or Ubers available, and even the buses weren't running. My only solution was to take off the shoes and proceed home barefoot.

It was at this moment—after I removed my shoes—that I really took stock of the unprecedented scene I was surrounded by. I was alone in Midtown Manhattan. Not a soul to be seen anywhere. And because nearly every business was shuttered, it was much darker than usual for New York City. The only illumination came from the eerie light of the full moon casting shadowy figures against the boarded-up businesses and apartments.

And the quiet. Absolutely no sounds other than the occasional siren from an emergency vehicle off in the distance. I felt like I had stumbled onto the set of *I Am Legend*. I half expected a zombie to emerge from one of the dark alleyways and contemplated how I would escape in my hobbled state.

I slowly made my way back toward my apartment, taking extreme care to avoid stepping on any of the usual treasures that litter the New York City sidewalks. Fortunately, between the rain and relatively idle state of the city, the sidewalks were unusually clean, and the full moon provided just enough light to avoid any major land mines.

As I neared my apartment, I noticed a group of police officers clustered around a barricade. This may be the moment where my costume would have to work its magic. But would it work? Could I really expect the officer to not ask for an explanation as to why I was barefoot and bloodied from working a shift at the local hospital? *Well, we're about to find out*, I thought to myself.

As I approached, the officer waived me over. "You know there's a curfew, right? Are you coming from work?"

"Yes, sir, officer. I just got off my shift," I muttered lowly so as not to blast him in the face with my booze breath. I had luckily timed my departure from Amy's just after 11:00 pm, which is when the hospital typically releases the evening shift.

"You sure you're okay? Your eyes look a little bloodshot."

I felt my pulse quicken. I was so distracted by the weirdness of my environment and by trying not to step on biomedical waste or dog shit that I neglected to notice that I had started transitioning from being drunk to being hungover.

"Um, yes, I'm fine," I stammered. "I worked a double shift today, and I haven't really slept much."

He must have been transfixed on my blossoming hangover, for he neglected to notice or mention my bare and bloody feet. I can also see from his face and his posture that he had been working a long shift. The constant social unrest night after night had likely resulted in a lot of long shifts for him, and I was hoping to take advantage of his fatigue and sneak through this checkpoint. A few more nerve-racking seconds passed before he grunted and waived me down my street. After a few hundred more yards of carefully playing hopscotch around few remaining hazards in my way, I finally reached my apartment. I ascended the stairs, and as soon as I entered, I promptly threw the shoes in the garbage.

There to greet me was my four-legged feline antagonist, who was belligerent over the lateness of her dinner.

After I deposited the requisite amount of meat pellets in her bowl, I noticed that she was staring at my feet.

"Don't fucking start with me. I've had a day," I spouted out flatly.

She looked up from my feet to make eye contact and then squinted judgingly. I began to devise further retorts to her poor attitude, but in my state of delirium, I can only mutter, "What, cat got your tongue?"

Disgusted at the ineptitude of my response and exasperated by losing a game of wits to an animal with a brain the size of a lemon, I turned and made a beeline down the long hall toward my bedroom, stopping only briefly in the bathroom to wash all of New York City off my feet. After peeling off my bat suit, I mercifully collapsed into bed and passed out into a deep, mescal-induced slumber.

Epilogue

Amy and I unfortunately didn't last very long. Dating in New York is daunting under normal circumstances. Amy saved me that day from another night of COVID-19 solitude, and with the help of an incredibly weird shutdown version of New York and a lot of booze, we were able to forget our problems and enjoy a wonderful time together. But she was not my forever person. After a few more dates, we both felt that the spark just wasn't there, and we amicably parted ways.

In one of the last posts that I saw on Amy's Instagram (before she unfollowed me), I saw her holding up a set of keys in what appeared to be a new apartment. It was only about six months since we had parted ways, and I felt such a sense of joy for her to finally be unstuck. I'm not sure exactly what had prompted her to finally push herself over the mental mountain that was preventing her from tackling her dreams without a partner. Maybe I had something to do with it, as I represented yet another promising relationship that ultimately lacked the key ingredients for a life partnership. Perhaps it was me and maybe a few more unsuccessfully relationships after me that finally pushed Amy to go for her goal alone. Regardless of why, I was so happy to see Amy move forward. As I'm writing this now, I hope that Amy has found her person and that they're making fabulous cocktails together in her new place.

Secretly, though, I was jealous of Amy. I still felt very stuck myself. Having lost so much in the early days of the pandemic, I was feeling unmoored; and I desperately wanted to find a grounding presence, an instigator to help me move forward in my pursuit of my own goals. Instead, I felt my own aloneness like an anchor, weighing me down and stagnating me in my own little place of sadness. I was obsessed with my quixotic quest, but unlike the uber-confident Don Quixote, I felt lost and directionless in how to precisely pursue it. Unfortunately, it would be several years before I would find the wisdom to define what my true quest was and even longer to find the courage to pursue it alone.

Nevertheless, the thirty-ninth birthday date is one that I'll never forget. I think that this particular story is rife with interesting reflections to be gleaned. Firstly, I think that this story highlights the importance of human resiliency and on not losing hope. That brief exchange with Amy was not what I was looking for, but it was exactly what I needed in the moment, and it was by destiny's benevolent hand that it was given to me at just the right time.

Amy imbued with me kindness, a kindness that was impervious to the anger, fear, and uncertainty that permeated the city around us. In a moment where I was at my lowest, a person who was nearly a perfect stranger to me extended me an infusion of compassion when I needed it most. It was a reminder that no matter how dark things seem, something amazing may be just around the corner. Even though Amy's presence in my life was fleeting, this lesson stuck with me for the months and helped me to get through the arduous times ahead during the first winter of the pandemic.

Amy's presence was also a critical reminder in aiming smaller. When one is on a quixotic quest for love, things can sometimes get blown out of proportion, and every date can take on a sense of unwarranted grandiosity. As destiny would have it, Amy's role in my life was not meant to be long term, but the significance of our encounter was in no way diminished by the brevity of our time together. I think that one of Amy's lessons was most definitely how to deescalate the stakes for dates and to just take what life has to offer rather than trying to bulldoze over experiences with a premediated agenda.

The last and perhaps most glaring lesson is to never again wear new fucking shoes on a date ever again. I mean, what the actual fuck was I thinking? I literally asked for this outcome to happen by tempting fate with my stupidity, and I'm lucky that I didn't end up in a jail cell as a result.

I suppose in reflecting on my ephemeral encounter with Amy, I think my takeaway word is "kindness." But it easily could also be "lucky." I was truly lucky to have a savior that rainy June 5 back in 2020, and my gratitude for her will be with me the rest of my life. If you're reading this, Amy, I just want to say, "Thank you."

CHAPTER 4

Learning Spanish from a Somm

What man can pretend to know the riddle of a woman's mind?

—Miguel de Cervantes

As someone who is not a morning person—and a chronic insomniac—I would sleep as long as possible and leave the bare minimum time to get ready in the morning when I was younger. As I aged, I developed this little ritual of taking time to read in bed before starting my day, even if it meant having to set the alarm a bit earlier. Over time, the cat has taken well to this routine; and most mornings, she joins me in bed to relax before her long day of napping and plotting my demise commences.

On this particular day in the early fall of 2020, I was struggling to read the *New York Times* on my phone as my temples throbbed from the hangover that spearheaded my morning. I was also struggling to hold the phone, as my injured finger was still unprotected from the prior night's adventure. Frustrated by my many sources of discomfort, I got up to grab some ibuprofen and stepped into a large patch of cat litter, which only increased my ire for this already very unfortunate Thursday.

While not a father yet myself, I do have a rambunctious niece, so I know how messy children can be. For those of you who have never had pets, let me tell you that living with a cat is like a scaled-down version of living with a child. She is a proficient and constant creator of messes. Between the hair, the litter, and the debris from her cardboard scratch pad, her presence mandates multiple vacuums per day. That is until I finally splurged on my one great pet owner life hack: a robot vacuum. On this aggravating Thursday morning, I promptly activated the vacuum on my way back to bed with a fresh cup of coffee.

Back in bed, I was reflecting on the night before and how I could notch another failure into my scorecard on the quixotic quest for true love. Sasha was not future wife. Indeed, she would not even be returning for a second date. I probably could have guessed that this would happen had I paid more attention to the context clues in her profile, or if I had just been more honest with myself and my true motivations for leaving my apartment the night before.

While I was trying to make sense of everything that had happened, my mind was distracted and kept returning to a phrase that my date has said repeatedly, "Que rico." I knew what it meant, having taken four years of high school Spanish, but in the context it was used the night prior, I was quite befuddled. As I was pondering this peculiar idiom, the robot vacuum popped and fizzed in the background as it rode over vast swaths of cat litter. I was about to search Urban Dictionary when I heard this scratching sound from under the bed, and as I turned my head, I saw the vacuum emerge dragging a large black bra.

At first, I was unclear if what I was seeing was real; it was only when I looked to see that the cat was also fixated on the scene that was unfolding did I realize this was actually happening. Her gaze turned slowly away from the vacuum—now wedged uselessly into the corner, bra still in tow—and gave me the greatest, "What the fuck, man?" look I've ever seen on a feline face. I met her stare and burst into laughter.

*****

Signing up for an intramural flag football team was one of the best things that I ever did in New York. I met some cherished friends through that league, and the regular exercise was helpful in blunting the inevitable middle-aged waist expansion that plagues many members of the over-forty club. Once the pandemic started, the leagues all officially shut down, but many of the players were undeterred. Every Saturday, a group of us from across the city would gather on Randall's Island to play in unsanctioned pickup games, and this particular Saturday was no exception.

Beleaguered and blinded by sweat, I sauntered back to the huddle with my hands on my hips. I glanced at my knee and saw the steady flow of blood down my shin matched the steady impulse of pain traversing to my tired brain, which was still baked in booze from the prior night's festivities. The game was late, the afternoon was dragging on, and as I was about ten years older than the players I was chasing, I was thoroughly exhausted. With only a handful of seconds left, the game hung in the balance. My squad was trailing by a score. I lurched forward to receive my instructions from my ramshackle quarterback. Rub the DB off the line, then hit the seam straight and fast, ending the route with a skinny post toward the middle of the end zone. Seemed simple enough, and it would be if I were about eight years younger. Regardless of my middle-aged physical ineptitude, this was the play; and the game was on the line, so try I must and try I shall.

In the blink of an eye, the play was live as I streaked in slow motion toward my instructed destination. I whipped my head around just in time to see the ball in flight toward me as my eyes grew wide. I lifted my hands, and as they made contact with the ball, I could feel my right pinky finger immediately shatter as I attempted to grip the leather with all my might. To further complicate matters, in my usual state of unawareness, I had also failed to notice that my teammate and I were on a direct collision course. As we smashed into each other head-on, the ball squirted free from my feeble grasp and fell gently into the caress of the artificial turf. As I lay on the ground, my face staring directly at the stitching on the side of the football and with a new pain coursing up my right arm, I wondered what the hell I was doing with my life.

While the post-football libations were effective in temporarily palliating the pain in my finger, by the next day, it was evident that I needed medical care. I was no stranger to sports injury, having broken my nose three times by the time I graduated high school and having two foot surgeries in my early twenties. But my latest predilection seemed to be breaking my fingers playing flag football, as this was my second one in as many years. One of my colleagues at the hospital, upon seeing my second finger cast, quipped if I might need to start taking calcium supplements to combat my early onset osteoporosis. Hilarious, just fucking hilarious.

But the quest for true love doesn't abate for damaged digits, and as long as one finger was still functional, I was still able to swipe. A few days after the accident, I was at home preparing dinner for the cat when my phone lit up from the coffee table. A die-hard righty, I reached for it with the best three fingers and thumb my now-less-than-dominant hand could give and balanced it precariously on the heel of my palm.

"You matched!" beamed at me from the lock screen.

Navigating to the app, eager to meet my future soul mate, I opened into a strikingly deep pair of sea-green eyes staring up at me. "Well, hello, Sasha," I murmured to myself.

Aside from her eyes, another striking feature about Sasha was how quickly she messaged, and she moved from small talk to suggesting we meet up with alacrity. She actually suggested that we meet up the next day for drinks, which was quite a departure from the usual too-busy New York City vibe. I appreciated how she was direct and to the point.

Despite her enthusiasm, I had questions about Sasha. Her profile did not reveal much about what she was looking for. The only major detail divulged was that she was currently employed as a sommelier at a high-end New York City steakhouse. My profile, on the other hand, was plastered with lots of details about my intentions and with words like "marriage, kids, settling down," etc. My hope was that this overt display of my quixotic quest to find true love would filter out those who were interested in other pursuits. Sasha's messages proved she was adept at brevity; she was also flirtatious and a little bit mysterious. I truly wasn't sure what she intended from this date that we were planning.

Speaking of planning, this was unfortunately going to have to be a date deferred, as I was going away on a short business trip the day after matching with Sasha. Usually, even a few days' delay in the first date is the kiss of death in New York dating, as I'm sure Sasha would match with twenty-five other suitors during my few days away from the city. Surprisingly, however, upon my return to the city, I reached out to Sasha; and she replied almost immediately that she was free to meet up the following night. Now I was really intrigued. Not only had she waited, but she was again free to meet on very short notice.

In the fall of 2020, dating in the city was still hazardous. While potential romance seekers were no longer required to walk and drink on the go, most of the seating options were still outdoors on the sidewalk. I selected a place on the corner of my street in Hell's Kitchen, a little Mexican spot named Anejo. This place had saved me many a night early in the pandemic, when grabbing to-go margaritas and in-house prepared guacamole was literally the only thing to do on a Friday night. On this fall evening, it was fortunately a little balmy, which allowed us to sit outside comfortably (at least from a temperature standpoint). I also found myself with nerves on the first date, which probably reflects the relative mystery surrounding Sasha at that point in our new relationship.

The place was a mere five hundred meters from my front door, so I was able to arrive early. Wedged at a small table with a drink to calm my nerves, I waited for Sasha. She arrived about ten fashionable minutes late and greeted me with a very vigorous hug and a kiss on the cheek.

Her outfit was a bit unusual, as she had clearly intended on taking every opportunity afforded to her by the unseasonably warm weather. She was donned in a light spring jacket, which thinly vailed a sleeveless crop top, and a very short skirt, which showed off her impressively athletic legs. She was shorter, about 5'1", with neatly trimmed brown hair that fell just above her shoulders. But what stood out were those eyes—those immersive, deep-green eyes. They had their own gravity, like a black hole; and once I was locked into them, it was almost hard to look away at times.

Our conversation started very nervously at first, and the waiter compassionately appeared to take our drink orders and to deposit a bowl of chips and salsa on the table. After the first round of margaritas arrived, we both settled into a more natural state of talking. As it would turn out, Sasha was born in Puerto Rico and moved to the US when she was about eight or ten years old. She spoke clean English with no accent, and with a name like Sasha, I was surprised to learn that she was not Russian. When I saw her name and pictures on the app, I was honestly expecting someone from Eastern Europe. This little surprise was quite romantic and added to her enigmatic allure.

Adding further to her mystery, I soon uncovered that she was not a sommelier, but rather, she was recently enrolled in classes for this profession. So she was presently, in fact, a waitress serving wine at a local wine bar.

Why the fib? I wondered.

After we had three rounds of margaritas and shared a half-dozen tacos, I drunkenly determined that we had been in one spot for the longest acceptable period of time for a first date and proposed that we move locations. She happily obliged, and we walked over one avenue to Ninth and found the only place open this "late" on a Wednesday.

Lily's Craft and Kitchen was the lone soldier still serving on Ninth, so that was where we posted up for our last drink out. We each ordered the house draft beer, which was a delicious take on a red ale. It was then that I finally understood her intentions for the evening (at least partially). Before we were halfway done with our ales, she leaned in to ask me, "So are we doing this or what?"

I was pretty sure I knew what she meant, but before I can ask for clarification, she skillfully took my hand off the table and glided it under her shirt into the small of her back. Fortunately, she had chosen the hand without the finger cast.

Well, here we go, I thought to myself.

We spun through the door of my apartment, already engrossed in the type of drunk make out that every New Yorker has seen around 2:00 a.m. in the corner of the bar as the lights turn on for last call.

We stumbled down the long hallway to my bedroom, and before I had much time to think, she was taking off my pants.

She had already discarded her shirt in the hallway, and the only article of clothing remaining was her pesky bra. I reached my right hand deftly behind her to unhook the damn thing, and as I did, my finger cast was caught. And as the bra sailed away into the darkness of the bedroom, my cast was attached firmly.

I shrieked in pain as my fractured digit was violently exposed by this unfortunate maneuver. Fortunately, Sasha was so plastered that she thought I was crying out with pleasure, so we didn't even miss a beat in our lovemaking, even as I was audibly choking back tears of agony.

Eventually, I composed myself, and we consummated the night. The sex was hot and primal, and Sasha was fully engrossed in our passionate affair—so engrossed, in fact, that she seemed to lose herself in repetition of the unlikely phrase, "Que rico," which she was yelling throughout.

Having taken many years of high school Spanish, I knew this term to mean, "How rich," as in something a grandmother would say in reference to a dessert. As Sasha kept saying it, I eventually got distracted trying to imagine which dessert I was. Was she calling me a cake, a pie, or maybe a cannoli? I was so obfuscated by her continued utterance of this phrase that I nearly lost my focus on the task at hand.

After a while, we eventually finished and collapsed into the deep sort of intoxicated postcoital sleep that is usually reserved for weddings and birthdays. The last thought that ran through my mind before I passed out was whether I should get up to search for my lost finger cast.

My next memory is of hearing the gentle ruffling of the sheets. As I awoke, I realized that I was sleeping with a T-shirt draped over my face for reasons I still don't understand, so I was unable to identify the sound at first. When I gently lifted the shirt to peer out, I can see Sasha's silhouette in the morning sun as she quietly gathered her belongings.

This was completely new territory for me. Why was she sneaking away in the wee hours of the morning? I had never had someone try to leave without saying goodbye. *I thought that we had had a good time the night before*, I wondered to myself. *What was she running from?*

The decision in this moment was whether I continue to pretend to be asleep, or I shatter the silence of this escape ritual with an awkward greeting of some sort. Then after a few seconds of pondering, I decided to keep still and let her finish sneaking out. I mean, what would I even have said? "Good morning?" "Where ya going?" "Want some coffee for the road?" I figured it better to leave her with whatever peace that she needed from exiting in such a way.

After enough time had passed that I was sure she was gone, I got up, stumbled down the hall, and flipped on the coffeepot.

Epilogue

If any of you reading this story have still not plugged "que rico" into Urban Dictionary yet, I'll spare you the trouble:

> Normally it mean delicious when refering to food. However, beware the phrase is also used during sex or climax in spanish. Usually by the girl.

> 1)   yes! yes! deeper! deeper! ummm que rico papi!
> 2)   person (A): we have smooth velvet cake for dessert!
>   person (B): yum que rico!

I certainly got a good chuckle when I finally did, and while Sasha didn't turn out to be my forever person, I very much appreciated the edification in Spanish language slang that I received that night.

A day or two after our date, I texted Sasha playfully about the missing item of clothing she had left behind. I was a bit surprised when she promptly messaged back that she had no interest in retrieving her bra or in seeing me again. She parted ways with me with the typical line, "I've got stronger connections with other people on the apps," and abruptly terminated any hope for a second date.

I was then again in unfamiliar territory, having now to dispose of a bra for the first time. I actually googled, "How to dispose a bra," and was pleased to find the information for a local women's shelter that was taking donations.

With the logistical issue of the extra clothing accessory now taken care of, I found myself reflecting on the strangeness of the whole encounter. Why had she pursued me so aggressively for a one-night stand? Why the fib about her job? Was her name even really Sasha?

As fate would have it, I would have to wait quite some time for my answer to these questions. About six months after my night with Sasha, Facebook abruptly submitted her profile to me a friend suggestion. I'm not sure how the algorithm connected us at first, but later, I figured it must be because we exchanged phone numbers. Her profile was surprisingly not protected, and I was able to easily peruse her pictures. From what I was able to glean, Sasha was either engaged or already married to another man!

Suddenly, everything made complete sense. The secrecy, the mystery, the abrupt disappearance after our night of "delicious" sex was all because she was probably already with someone else.

My mind began to swirl as I attempted to digest this new information. I had never been a party to extracurricular activities like this before, and the feelings that I had about it were not good. While I certainly was not an altar boy, I was a God-fearing Catholic, thanks to my ex-wife; and I initially felt a strong sense of guilt over having participated in such an act of relationship betrayal.

My encounter with Sasha taught me several lessons. First, I learned to be more trusting of my instincts. My spider senses were tingling early in the date, and I ignored my intuition and took things at face value rather than digging deeper. That was not a mistake that I intended to repeat. As a simple Midwestern boy, my default approach was always to take people for their word without question until they give me a reason not to. And I think that most people like to be a bit mysterious early on in relationships, as this can add a little intrigue and perhaps heighten the sexual tension that customarily percolates in this early phase of dating. However, there is a line between being mysterious and flat out lying, and my night with Sasha taught me to not be so intrinsically trusting of new people that I meet online.

Sasha did hide things from me, but I'm not blameless in this encounter. She didn't put any info on her profile regarding what she was looking for, but I also didn't ask. I'm certainly not averse to casual sex. I mean, it's fun right? But it's also not what I'm looking for primarily, and by simply asking a few questions about what Sasha was looking for, I may have avoided a deviation from the quest that happened to put me in bed with someone else who was already spoken for. So lesson learned there: stay true to the quest.

Despite the obvious tainting that comes with learning that Sasha was likely spoken for, I still have a somewhat fond memory of that night. The sex was deeply passionate and fiery hot, and after being with her, I was reminded that this was the level of passion that I would seek to find in my forever partner. And despite the fibbing, I still think that she was a nice person.

Still, I spent a lot of time wondering why she did it. Was she unhappy in the relationship? Were they just fighting at the time, and she needed an escape? Perhaps she never intended it to go that far and only decided to go for it once we were drunk. Perhaps she was a confused or ambivalent about her relationship, and maybe through her encounter with me, she was able to gain clarity about her situation and make the decision to move forward with something more serious with her partner. Of the available options, that's the one that I like to imagine, anyway.

In the end, I decided if I truly were a God-fearing person, then forgiveness was the only way forward; and I decided to show compassion for Sasha and hope that she was in a better place wherever she was. Learning (and relearning) to show compassion to others is really the yeast in the bread when it comes to building successful relationships. After going through the rigors of the pandemic, this little exercise with Sasha was very useful in reminding me of the importance of being compassionate and forgiving with myself and my potential forever partners.

So my word for Sasha is "passion." But it obviously could also be "compassion."

And, Sasha, if you're out there reading this, I just want to say, "God bless and Godspeed."

C H A P T E R   5

A Heated Affair

For hope is always born at the same time as love.

—Miguel de Cervantes

Veronica and I approached the corner of Fifty-Eighth and Ninth, which is where I would have to stop holding her hand. She looked so smart and yet so cute in her circular glasses and her snug beanie, which framed her face just perfectly.

"When will I see you again?" I asked impetuously.

"Not sure. I think a few weeks and we'll be done with all of this," she replied as her eyes drifted slowly to the pavement.

The tension was palpable in this unwanted goodbye. With the city now completely closed and the hospitals heaving with the sick and the dying, there was no longer a reason for her to remain.

"I'm going to miss you," I sputtered.

"You haven't known me long enough to say that."

She was right, of course. We had only known each other a few weeks. And however memorable they were, I found myself wondering if I really would miss her or whether I was just really sad that she was the last semblance of my life before the pandemic to disappear.

"We'll stay in touch while you're away, yeah?" I replied.

"Of course, hun," she quipped back as she tucked Lucy under her arm.

Although it was brief, I had really enjoyed having them both Veronica and her white Coton de Tulear Lucy quarantine with me. And the cat had very much enjoyed having an animal in the apartment that was smaller than her. I think that she might miss Lucy just as much as I'll miss Veronica.

In my heart, I somehow knew that this was likely the last time that I would see her. The sense of foreboding that flooded over the city had not spared us. I suppose this feeling was a combination of the end of the world that was before the pandemic, along with all the uncertainty that awaited us all going forward. When I looked back up at her, I could sense that she felt it too.

"While I'm stuck in quarantine, I'll be thinking about *Come from Away*," I said as I immediately began blushing.

The cool March breeze whipped through us, and with our feelings already laid bare on that gloomy, gray street corner, I felt like I were being stripped to the bone by the sadness of this moment.

"So will I," she replied with a big smile as she leaned in and kissed my cheek.

After a few seconds that felt like hours, she finally turned and walked eastward on Fifty-Eighth. I stood for a long time on that street corner until I couldn't see her anymore, and the cold reality that I was going to have to face this pandemic by myself going forward set in. I finally turned around and headed back to my apartment.

I feel like every time the New Year comes around, all I see on social media is the same old shit. "This is finally going to be my year." Famous last words I've always thought. For me, at least, the last several years since I'd moved to New York had not "finally been my year." Sure, work was going well; and I was making new friends, exploring the city, going on weekend jaunts to Europe, etc. But I still felt emotionally (and perhaps spiritually) stuck. Despite my divorce, my heart still longed to find a partner. And so with each drop of the ball on New Year's Eve since I had moved to New York City, my quixotic quest for love remained unfulfilled.

Especially with how badly dating had gone in 2019, I was really hoping for things to improve. Early into 2020, however, I truly believed that it might finally be my year. Obviously, a huge shitstorm would explode out of nowhere that March that would ensure that 2020 was in fact no one's year. But let's not reflect on that steaming geyser of misery right now, dear reader, and instead focus on the good ole times before the pandemic.

Living alone in New York is just expensive, period. I also wanted to live in Midtown, and I refused to share a studio with the cat, as I had no desire to be exposed to her nocturnal predilections for howling into the darkness after she goes level-ten feral at 2:00 a.m. I also reasoned that having a one-bedroom apartment would make more attractive to potential mates, as it certainly was a status symbol to have so much space without any (human) roommates. So with the price of a one bedroom being what it was at the time, I had no choice but to work various side hustles to make ends meet.

The most lucrative of these was my consulting venture, which was colloquially named "The Heart Smart PharmD." Basically, I had convinced a few pharmaceutical companies that I knew my shit and that it was worth their time and money to fly me to destinations and have me pitch their product over lunch or dinner to other health-care providers. I had been slowly building my name since 2016, and at the start of 2020, things were taking off. I had the entire last week of March booked up to hit three cities on the west coast—all expenses paid—with a take-home purse that was north of $10,000. Not bad money for one week's effort.

Adding to this, my friends and I had found a way to scheme a trip to Budapest for a week's long conference in April that we were able to write off on our taxes as a work expense. Free trip to Europe with five of my best friends? Yes, please!

Indeed, everything was falling into place with work and friends. I certainly felt like for the first time in a while that I had the wind at my back. And then I met Veronica.

Veronica was a very interesting hit on Bumble. Her pictures were lovely if not unassuming. She appeared to be standard Americana, with brown hair to match her eyes and a smile that felt very Midwestern. As pleasant as her profile was, there was nothing outstanding about it, which is tough to overcome in the sea of New York City exceptionalism.

There were lots of pictures of travel on Veronica's page, and I certainly enjoyed seeing that we enjoyed the same spots—Amsterdam, Belgium, and London, just to name a few. However, most people in New York have passports, and being well-traveled here is not a particularly noteworthy feature. I was actually about to swipe left on Veronica and close the door on our would-be romance before it began.

As I continued down her profile past her pictures, I noticed she had connected her Spotify playlists to her Bumble account, and I was able to see a few similarities. *Lots of emo/indie pop, definitely a good sign*, I thought to myself. So I kept scrolling and then I saw that her Instagram account was also connected to her Bumble. Jackpot.

What I saw was a whole different side of Veronica. Through her videos and photos, I learned that she was a performer! The reason she was traveling so much is because she actually performed on cruise ships once upon a time, and she was very talented as both a singer and dancer. There was a video of her singing a beautiful impromptu performance of "Seven Nation Army" by the White Stripes!

As someone who is very left-brained, I've always had a soft spot for artists. I'm atrocious at anything remotely artistic. Even my handwriting is mostly illegible. I can remember all throughout elementary school receiving "needs improvement" on every report card when it came to my cursive. So while I can easily balance organic chemistry equations, I couldn't probably draw a stick figure rendition of myself and the cat if someone had a gun to my head and my life depended on it. So yeah, Veronica's artistic qualities were taking effect on me quite quickly.

Her artistic qualities notwithstanding, Veronica was also hot. The photos on her social media were much clearer than the blurry images on her Bumble page. Her dance videos, in particular, put her sensuality on full display. There was this one video in particular, which just floored me. It was shot in black and white, and Veronica was shimmying forward, hips and shoulders bopping in unison, staring directly into the camera. Her outfit spared little for the imagination, and she had the toned physique that comes from years of semiprofessional dancing. Needless to say, I couldn't swipe right fast enough.

As luck would have it, we quickly matched! It was then that the terrifying tick of the clock began, for on Bumble, the women have twenty-four hours from matching to message the men. If she does not open the chat, the match would expire, and our opportunity for love would close forever. And I cannot reach out first. There's nothing I can do. So while I had done my part to thwart the capricious hand of fate by doing my deeper dive into Veronica's profile, I was now at the mercy of fate once again.

Fortunately, she opened the chat with a perfunctory "Hi!" and our adventure began. Our conversation flowed effortlessly on Bumble, and we quickly exchanged numbers and started planning to meet. Veronica seemed like a very promising match, and when I have a very promising match, I usually try to do something unique for the first date. As she was a performer, I knew that I must integrate the theater somehow. I managed to secure us last minute tickets to *Come from Away*. Needless to say, the idea was a hit.

We didn't have much time to talk during the play, but despite the brevity of our time knowing each other, she sat very close to me through the whole performance, and we held hands numerous times. It was very sweet in all honesty.

In the conversation that ensured after the show, I really got to see the real Veronica for the first time. She was passionate about performing arts, and her journey to New York City was the culmination of her dream. She told me stories about waking up at 4:00 a.m. or 5:00 a.m. to be the first one standing in line at various casting auditions across the city and stories of the constant rejection that accompanies this pursuit of a dream. To see her face light up when she spoke of landing her first big break, it was hard not to be enthralled, even though her first break was far from actually being big. I must admit that I had my concerns before the date that perhaps our very different backgrounds would hinder our conversations. However, I think that shared interests tend to come second to shared passions and that a passionate pursuit of one's dream profession is a language that requires no translation.

I'm not entirely sure if the genesis of my connection with Veronica was due to our shared pursuit of our passion or from our steadfast desire to escape from Midwestern mediocrity. Veronica spoke of a hometown very much like my own, one mired in the rust belt after the decline of American manufacturing. It seemed that we both reveled in escaping that bleak future for bigger dreams in New York City. Regardless of how it started, there was definitely a connection there to pursue. I made sure to secure a second date before walking her to the train station that evening.

*****

As soon as we entered the studio, I realized that I had made a critical error.

The first and inescapable sensory assault was the stench. It was a literal punch in the nose, as my eyes almost started to water as I passed through the precipice of the front door. It was like sweat caked on more sweat, all layered onto a sweat-soaked gym sock burrito of sweat.

I've been a regular at yoga studios for over ten years, and I've never smelled anything like this. When I signed up for this random $20 class pass, I didn't notice the details of what I exactly I was signing up for. As I spoke to the receptionist and she read me the mandatory health waiver, I could feel the heat wafting out from the back room where the class would take place.

After signing eighteen health clearance forms, I was handed a towel so tiny that it was almost ceremonial. As I entered the studio room, my skin was blasted with a suffocating 105-degree blast of air. Even on my travels in India, I had not encountered such a heavy, humid, oppressive blanket of heat. My entire body immediately erupted into perspiration.

What the holy hell was I doing here? And on a second date no less. After only a few steps into the studio, my eyes were stinging from the deluge of sweat streaking down my face. I used my ceremonial towel to wipe my brow once and immediately wished I was somewhere else.

That is, until Veronica and I settled into the corner near the front of the room. It was February, so I could feel a lifeline of frosty winter air creeping in slowly through an aged New York windowpane. I placed my mat as close to the window as possible, almost to the point that I could feel the cold air tickling my feet as I went through my cursory stretches.

I looked over at Veronica, and she was glistening with the precision of a professional dancer. The one plus of the extreme heat was that it had compelled her to remove her T-shirt, and she was set to practice in just her sports bra. This little gift was just enough to momentarily lift me from my heat-induced misery. I had to be careful not to get caught watching the beads of sweat make the downward trek over the tiny mountains of her abdominal muscles.

Fortunately, the class was also completely packed, so we were forced to separate our mats by only a few inches. Amid the sea of sweat and heat that was oppressing my senses, I was able to get a few merciful whiffs of her floral perfume. Her luscious scent was the perfect distraction from the odious heat and even made me temporarily forget the perfidious website that had concealed from me that this was in fact a hot yoga class.

Despite this grotesque environment, I was an experienced yogi, and I expected to be able to survive this class unscathed. We began the practice doing sun salutations, and the pace quickly hastened. Poses were held for barely a half of a breath as the militant little instructor belted out commands for increasingly harder poses. It soon seemed that her intent was on ensuring that I drop dead from heatstroke before ever getting to finish this date.

By now, my mat was completely soaked in sweat, and it was actually starting to get slippery. *This is bat-shit crazy*, I thought to myself. *I might actually fly off this mat and kill someone nearby if she doesn't slow down with these poses.*

Then a fateful mistake. I was attempting to transition from a standing warrior pose down to a seated twist, and I actually slipped. I think that I managed to catch myself before Veronica saw anything, as she was already in the twist and facing away from me. But I felt a funny pinch in my lower back as I struggled to regain my posture. I didn't really think anything of this sensation at the time, but little did I know that I had just pulled the pin on a live grenade.

The class eventually ended after an hour or so of hell that would make a stay at the Hanoi Hilton look like a luxury resort. The torture wasn't finished, however, for it was February; and we now had to exit the studio—caked in sweat—onto a subfreezing New York City sidewalk. *Just great,* I thought to myself. *I get to die simultaneously from heatstroke and frostbite.* These are the things we do for the quest for true love.

Veronica and I eventually found a warm bar and settled in for some hard-earned libations. After sharing a few drinks, we left the bar and then shared our first kiss before parting ways at the subway platform. In spite of all that had occurred (and all my mental complaining), I ended up having a great time, and I couldn't wait to see her again.

Our third date—which happened a few days after our second— was actually impromptu. I was supposed to be doing a consulting gig for the Heart Smart PharmD in the city, and it fell through at the last minute due to the early onset of pandemic restrictions. As luck would have it, Veronica was in the neighborhood and happened to text me as I was about to head home from my failed work endeavor. Instead of heading home to give the cat a full spa treatment, I met Veronica up for a drink.

We met at a crowded bar near Lincoln Center. The name escapes me now, but Veronica was seated already in the back, waiting for me as I entered. I was wearing a suit; and when she complemented me on it in her sly, subtle way, I could feel blood diverting into the small vessels of my cheeks and into larger vessels…elsewhere. She was dressed casually, having just finished teaching a dance class that night close to Lincoln Center.

After we shared some drinks and witty banter, I could feel her playing footsie with me under the table. She had kicked off her shoe and was moving her foot up and down on my leg. At this point, I had a hunch that the cat wasn't getting her nails trimmed that night.

We did in fact head back to my place promptly after the second drink, and it wasn't long after arrival before we were making our way down the long hallway. Our clothes came off quickly, and after a few moments of passionate kissing, Veronica belted out, "Fuck me, please!"

Fuck me, please. So hot yet so polite. I don't think I'll ever forget that phrase as long as I live. I gladly obliged. As I stood up, I grabbed her arms and pulled her up. I spun her around, and I was set to take her from behind; the live grenade went off.

Let me pause for a moment and explain the concept of old man back (OMB). My friend Al, one of the pharmacists whom I work with (who is also middle-aged), first introduced me to the concept. Al told me this story once of how he was mowing the lawn, and as he knelt down to pull the starter, he felt the pin slip out of his live grenade. Unlike me, he was experienced with OMB, so he knew he was now on borrowed time. He attempted to get into the house immediately but to no avail. His grenade went off on the front lawn, and he immediately collapsed. He could not get himself up, and his wife eventually found him and recruited a neighbor to lift Al up and take him inside.

Don't worry, Al is fine. OMB is temporary, and after a few days' convalescence, one can recover from OMB and live a relatively normal life. Unfortunately, though, once the grenade goes off, there's little hope for full functionality for the next few days at least.

So at this point, as I was standing behind the naked body of this beautiful woman, my back seized up. I actually felt my knees buckle as I struggled to regain my balance. I bit my lip to avoid shrieking in pain this time, although I'm not really sure how effective I was. I was in the full grip of OMB, and it was not letting me push forward to finish the task at hand.

At this point, I did the only thing I could think of. Rather than drive forward with my hips, like a young and virile version of myself, my OMB and I lurched forward; and I put my body weight onto Veronica. Thank god she was strong enough to hold us both up. Had she not been in such great shape, this maneuver would have certainly failed, and we would have both ended up on *Untold Stories from the E.R.*, trying to explain how this particular sex-related debacle occurred.

After a few brief moments of feigning fornication from behind, I was able to get my old ass onto the bed, and mercifully, she assumed control and got on top of me. In my supine state, I was able to consummate our first night together but only barely. Veronica fell asleep shortly after we finished, and I hobbled into the bathroom and hoovered a handful of anti-inflammatories and muscle relaxers before returning to spoon her for the rest of the night.

Veronica and I continued seeing each other for the next several weeks, but it was not long after our third date that things started to really close down. Veronica, Lucy, the cat, and I spent some lovely evenings quarantining together in my apartment. In the moment, I could not know how precious those moments would be for me, as they would some of the last happy ones that I would have for quite some time.

Then came the fateful morning. With the city completely shuttered, there was no demand for anyone to sing or dance on Broadway (or in any theater for that matter). In hard times like these, Veronica had always had backup options working as a waitress or barista, but these avenues for revenue were obviously closed as well. It was a cold March morning, a Sunday, when we were set to say our goodbye. Veronica was heading back home for a while to stay with her family and wait this thing out.

We spent a long time that morning hanging out in my living room. I can still remember sitting next to her on my couch, with her laptop perched on her perfect lap. She was asking for my advice about something, and for the life I me, I can't remember now what it was. I think I was distracted by the fact that I knew she was leaving. Also, I couldn't help but watch the cat and Lucy having another epic stare down in the kitchen over the water bowl, each waiting for the other to blink. I really enjoyed their cute little companionship. To this day, I'm still thinking about getting a small dog as a companion for the cat because of what I saw with Lucy.

Eventually, the time came for her to depart. We gathered our things, and as I put on my coat, she said, "You don't have to walk me down."

"I insist," I said.

And with that, we descended from my fourth floor walkup and headed north on Ninth Avenue.

Epilogue

I did see Veronica once more after our laconic goodbye, although it was until later in the summer of 2020. She had popped back into town for a visit with her friends, and we arranged to meet up for lunch.

We had not, in fact, kept in touch. My life descended into madness shortly after she left and the pandemic raced through New York in the spring of 2020, so I was completely unable mentally and emotionally to reach out meaningfully. I had such a tailwind heading into 2020. Fresh off my *Great Gatsby* New Year's party, everything was finally falling into place. She did eventually reach out to politely let me know that she was seeing someone new, a fact which I had astutely observed already from her Instagram account.

COVID-19 had destroyed it all. My lucrative consulting business? Gone. The amazing trip with my friends? Gone. And finally meeting someone great in New York, after the epic disaster that was my love life in 2019, only to have it snatched away before it even got started? Well, that was the proverbial straw. I was utterly devastated, and this string of losses would finally push me to the brink.

I did hold onto the memories of my brief encounter with Veronica for quite some time in the pandemic. Those first few weeks were so dark, and it just felt like we the health-care providers were at war. I imagined how soldiers in wars of the past must have clung to the memories of their girls back home when the shells were falling all around them. After some time, though, I found myself ruminating on Veronica too much. Especially into the early summer of 2020, I found myself having a hard time holding on to the memories of her. *Was she just the anchor for me to the era before COVID-19? I would wonder. "Was it really her that I was missing, or was it my life before COVID-19 that I was really longing for?"*

After some time, I realized that part of why I struggled to let go was because Veronica was the only relationship of mine that ended without either party consenting to it. In all my previous relationships, either one or both parties were ready to part ways. When relationships end that way, even though it's usually painful, I think it brings a sense of closure to things that I didn't feel like I got with Veronica. I felt cheated, cheated by the world and cruel hand of fate that ruined my perfect year before it ever got started.

At some point over the summer or fall, I noticed that Veronica had posted that she had met her new fella on the Brooklyn Bridge in early March, around the same time that she and I were seeing each other. I actually took a bit of peace from this little epiphany because what it meant was that she and I were not going to work out either way. From her posts, it seemed like she had a much stronger connection with this guy, and so the pandemic likely didn't alter our trajectory as much I had originally thought.

Regardless of this realization about Veronica, my mental health would eventually decline throughout the summer of 2020. I was fraught with episodes of anxiety that was uncontrollable at times, and these attacks would leave me shaking at my kitchen table, unable to think or move. My sleep was suffering, and I was significantly impaired in my ability to work effectively. I did reach out twice, once to a psychiatrist and another time to a counselor. The shrink told me that all my problems were self-inflicted, and I should start my road to recovery by completely abstaining from alcohol (which was shocking, as I was barely drinking during the pandemic since everything was closed). And the counselor told me that I shouldn't feel sad about being alone because "I was married once already." Barf. I ended my time with both of them after one or two sessions each. Due to these disastrous encounters, I would suffer with untreated mental health issues for nearly two more years.

One lesson that I did (eventually) learn from Veronica was that I needed to insulate myself more effectively from the outside world. I felt very victimized by the pandemic, as it wrestled control of my life away from me. I had let this victim mindset take hold of me, and it was fueling my already high anxiety that was already stemming from the pandemic. I think that it's a very basic lesson we hear as kids to not worry about the things that you can't control. Putting that into practice, however, was a real struggle for me for the remainder of 2020—and sadly, into 2021.

My lunch with Veronica in the summer of 2020 was uneventful. The conversation was so prosaic that I can't even remember what we discussed. It was strange to see her again having been through our own respective pandemic experiences. I had already gotten my closure from following her Instagram, so this meeting was just a pleasant one between old acquaintances. After we parted ways again that day after lunch, I never saw her again.

In reflecting on my time with Veronica and of how I grew after the encounter, I think my takeaway word is "resilience." But it easily could also be "hope." Thinking about holding her again after she left gave me a lot of hope in those early days of the pandemic, and for that, I'll always be grateful. So, Veronica, if you're out there reading this, I just want to say, "Thank you."

CHAPTER 6

A Date with Rocky Balboa

Truly I was born to be an example of misfortune, and a
target at which the arrows of adversary are aimed.

—Miguel de Cervantes

In my early forays into dating in New York, I almost exclusively
used the apps. These were the best—and only—options that I had at my
disposal at the time. In the start of 2016, however, that changed with an
innocuous sounding email from some company called "Modern Love
Club." From the name, I wasn't sure at first what made it "modern," and
I honestly thought it was some club for swingers. While I was intrigued
by the idea of swinging, I was still hell-bent on my quixotic quest for
true love, so diverting my dill pickle to dillydally in an informal love
dalliance was not something that really piqued my interest.

Despite my initial instinct to just delete the email, my curiosity
got the best of me, and I opened it. It was indeed from a matchmak-
ing service and appeared like a legitimate offer to come audition to
join their stable of men. They had spotted me on Match.com, and
they said based on my profile, I would make a good addition to their
rolodex of guys ready to be served up to eligible female bachelorettes.
Honestly, I was extremely flattered but still a little bit suspicious.

Modern Love Club didn't have much of a website in 2016, and
the address that they invited me to was a converted office suit in an

apartment building around Union Square. I wasn't super new to the city at that time, but I was definitely still a little green, and so I wasn't entirely thrilled about showing up to this makeshift office alone. Rather than take someone, I actually arranged a safety check-in with my coworker Nick. His dad was a cop, so he seemed like the logical choice. My appointment to meet the matchmaker was at 6:00 p.m., and I told Nick that if he didn't hear from me by 7:00 p.m., then he should assume I was in a basement bathtub somewhere in the bowels of Brooklyn missing a kidney.

In the interlude between making my appointment with the matchmaker and the day of our visit, I had a new match (my first on Bumble, actually) with a girl named Marcelle. As coincidence would have it, the only evening our schedules aligned was the same night as my matchmaker appointment. *No matter*, I thought. This is a nice opportunity to double-dip on the evening. I told Marcelle that I was already going to be in Union Square (for work, of course), and she promptly booked us a table at a bar in the area.

The matchmaker appointment was actually very painless—just a series of interview-style questions about me, my dating preferences, hobbies, etc. It was a pretty sweet gig, actually. I paid them nothing, and they did all the work of arranging a date with me and their clients. I just had to show up and be my charming self. Near the end of the visit, the matchmaker actually busted out a binder full of profiles and started showing me some clients.

I was impressed! These were attractive, successful women: doctors, lawyers, accountants, etc. And of them were also looking for true love—at least per the profiles. It seemed like I had stumbled onto a bonanza.

After I finished with the matchmaker, I scurried over to the bar, deftly evading the busy sidewalks full of people during the rush hour of Union Square. It was February and quite cold but that hadn't stop patrons from the area from flooding the bars for happy hour. When I arrived, I was glad that my date had booked us a table, as the place was already full.

Marcelle arrived just on time. She was actually quite pretty— Petite, around 5'2", with a deep tan that stood out from the pastiness that me and most of the other New Yorkers donned that time of the year. She has beautiful big blue eyes and dark curly hair that ended just at her mid back. She greeted me with a quick "hello," and we pressed ourselves against the hostess's stand in an attempt to get her attention amid the chaos.

Unfortunately, our table had been mistakenly given away to another couple. Marcelle wasn't angry, but she was deeply annoyed, and she was not restrained in expressing herself to the hostess. Her style of firm directness was not something that I would have ever been comfortable using, and as I would only come to find out about two years later, this was an important clue about Marcelle that I missed.

After the dust settled and we eventually got a different table, Marcelle and I settled into a lovely conversation. Despite her name, she was not French. In fact, she was Jewish and hailed from the verdant pastures of northern New Jersey. I was surprised at how easy it was to talk to her and how much our sense of humor matched up. I had been online dating in the city for roughly six months to this point, and this was certainly the most naturally comfortable date that I had been on since my divorce.

The interesting moment in the date came when I went downstairs to use the bathroom. I did my business, and as I spun around after exiting the men's room, I saw a painting on the wall that caught my eye. The reason that I have not named the bar that we were at that night in this book is because of this painting.

I know that what I saw could not be true. The person in this picture must be someone else. Who, I can't imagine. But to my eyes—and I was only one drink in at this point—the picture was a full-frontal portrait of Adolf Hitler.

I stared at this painting for way too long. I knew that it had to be someone else, some doppelgänger of Hitler, whom the management had thought it would be wise to enshrine right outside the men's room. I was honestly at a loss for words; and eventually, after several minutes, I had to break away from his fascist stare and go back upstairs. "What the literal fuck?" I muttered on the ascent. "Ending up on a date with a Jewish girl in a bar with a picture of Hitler in the basement." Inconceivable.

I rebounded from my astonishment and enjoyed another drink with Marcelle. It was then after we had shared some appetizers that she announced that she had to use the restroom. I jumped up and shrieked, "No!" only to startle myself with the volume of my voice.

"I mean," I said as I lowered my voice and attempted to recover from shrieking in a crowded happy hour bar, "when I was down there earlier, I saw that the ladies' room was out of order. Let's go somewhere else nearby for a nightcap."

Thankfully, she obliged, and we walked down the street to finish our evening. Even though our date was way back in 2016, I can still remember how we both had a great time and that we shared our first kiss that night. A second date was quickly booked the following day.

The second date went splendidly, and the third date was quickly on the books. Marcelle invited me over to her place for dinner, a sure-fire sign that she was serious about us. I arrived at the chosen hour, bottle of wine dutifully in hand, and we shared a lovely home-cooked meal together. As much as we were enjoying each other's company, one of the main topics of the evening was Felix, a cat that Marcelle had just adopted. Marcelle was a home health worker in the city, and she had been visiting a poor family in the Bronx that week. Felix was a rescue they had taken in during a recent snowstorm, and the family was not able to support him. When he jumped right into Marcelle's lap, the family asked her if she wanted him, and she obliged happily.

I did not have my cat at this point in my New York journey, but I grew up around cats, so I knew my way around these creatures. Felix was indeed friendly, and he jumped on my lap as we sat on the couch enjoying our after-dinner beverages. He insisted on being pet and bounced around between our laps until we were both covered in his fur.

It was probably around this time that I started to unconsciously rub my eyes. I had always been mildly allergic to cats, but when one has a cat, one tends to get slightly desensitized to such mild irritations. Once I had adopted my own cat, I had taken to consuming Benadryl every night to combat the allergies. However, at this time in my life, I hadn't lived with a cat in over ten years, and I was perhaps more susceptible than I realized in the moment. In this moment, however, I wasn't really paying attention to the cat, as Marcelle was leaning in close to me. She eventually started kissing my neck, which quickly turned into a heavy make out session. Before long, we were both groping each other, and she got up quickly to excuse herself for the bathroom.

After she left, I sat on the couch, barely able to restrain my excitement. I was already a little bit crazy for Marcelle, and this was leading up to my first-time having sex since my divorce. I was stoked that it wasn't with someone random and rather with someone I could definitely see dating going forward. And unfortunately, I was probably just inebriated enough to not notice that I was continuing to fuss with my right eye the whole time she was in the bathroom.

She eventually emerged, now only wearing a tight white blouse and her purple thong. Her tiny waist was peeking out from under her blouse, and her legs looked incredible for someone who's only form of exercise was walking to the subway and back.

"Did you come here to fuck me?" she asked as her blue eyes were flashing out from the darkness of the bedroom.

"Why, I absolutely did," I responded as I stood up and relieved myself of my cumbersome clothing.

Marcelle had positioned herself against her dresser, and as I approached from behind her, I saw my reflection in the mirror. What I saw was not great.

My right eye was very swollen, like freshly punched swollen. I was actually shocked that I could still see out of the bloody thing. Although to be fair, I was a little drunk at this point, so maybe I really was blind in the one eye and I didn't realize it. Either way, I knew I had to act fast in the unbelievable event that she hadn't see the lachrymose lesion that now dotted my right eye.

Marcelle was petite, so I quickly spun her around, picked her up, and threw her onto the bed. She actually giggled and laughed at this little WWE maneuver, and it seemed that for the moment in the darkness of the bedroom, my problematic pupil may go unnoticed.

Despite my blossoming ocular obstruction, Marcelle and I could consummate a beautiful first night together. Afterward, Marcelle was sharing her dreams of getting married, starting a family, and settling down in the next year or two. All this was music to my ears. Things were going very well, at least they were until I went into the bathroom to liberate my bladder from the wine from earlier.

When I saw myself again, this time in her bathroom mirror, my eye was completely shut, like "Cut me, Mick!" level closed. I was in the midst of the worst allergy attack that I'd had in years on the third night of a budding new romance.

My mind started racing for possible solutions. I was supposed to be at work the following day, so I quickly rationed that I could make an excuse that I needed to return home to be able to make my shift on time. To this point in the evening, even though the right side of my face looked like it was run over by a dump truck, she had not mentioned my eye at all. After finishing in the bathroom, I offered my pathetic excuse for leaving, which I felt terrible for as we had just had sex for the first time. She graciously accepted my excuse and encouraged me to head home promptly.

Once home, I ingested an ungodly amount of Benadryl and passed out quickly. Upon awaking the next day, my eye was still nearly closed. *Goddamn*, I thought. *That cat really did a number on me.* I toyed with the idea of suggesting to Marcelle that she change his name to Rocky or Creed.

There was no way that I could show up for work on a transplant floor looking like that. Anything related to the eye could be infectious. So I would have been sent home if I had tried to go to work. I finally decided to call in sick—for the next two days, actually. I missed two days of work because of my allergy to my soon-to-be girlfriend's cat.

Despite everything that happened that evening, Marcelle never once brought up my eye. That moment of classy kindness was never lost on me, even in spite of all the turmoil that was to follow eventually follow in our relationship.

Epilogue

I found it bitterly ironic that on the night I met with the matchmaker, I ended up meeting Marcelle. The matchmaker did reach out eventually with some potential dates, but by that third date with Marcelle, I was hooked, and I quickly dismissed the matchmaker and told her that her services were no longer required.

Marcelle and I continued dating, and soon, we were exclusive. After dating for four months, I had broken the lease on my rent-stabilized apartment, sold all my furniture to a charity from Cameroon that I found on Craigslist, and moved in with Marcelle. A few months later, we were engaged, and we married just after a year of meeting.

Needless to say, such an impetuous series of decisions did not end well. I had barely been divorced from my first wife a year when I met Marcelle, and she was the first person that I dated seriously after divorce number one. By November of 2017, our marriage was in shambles, as the foundation-building part of the relationship was completely skipped over. A hasty separation soon ensured, followed by a relatively easy divorce (New Jersey and Florida have that in common). As with my first divorce, we had no kids and owned no property, so there were very little material assets to squabble over. The sad, sardonic twist to the situation is that when I needed to find an apartment quickly after separating from Marcelle, I ended up right back where I had landed after my first divorce: hospital housing in Washington Heights.

This circuitous path back to hospital housing following the marital crash and burn should have forced a hard stop for me and my dating life. I should have taken a serious amount of time to evaluate myself and my life. What I know now, years later having done the critical work in therapy, is that the true motive for my quixotic quest had become tainted. Or perhaps it's more accurate to say—thinking back to my childhood—that it may have been tainted all along.

What happened with Marcelle was tragic for many reasons. For starters, I only found out post-divorce that all my family and friends hated her. You see, her demeanor when addressing the hostess was a clue that I missed on the first date, one which was pointing to the fact that Marcelle was quite a bitch sometimes—mostly to other people, rarely if ever to me, which is probably why I missed it the whole time we were together. She was actually very kind to me most of the time.

On our honeymoon in Greece, for instance, my OMB blew out again; and she went through heroic efforts to get the resort to bring us a heating pad. While we asked for a heating pad, what we got was a blue gel thing that had to be heated in the microwave. As soon as I laid on it, the damn thing exploded; and afterward, our honeymoon bed looked like Papa Smurf has just blown a huge load of cum everywhere. It was both funny and tragic. But Marcelle never got upset, never complained. She was very loving and supportive throughout the whole trip despite my old man ailments.

Meanwhile, my poor sister eventually revealed that she had to take Xanax around the clock whenever Marcelle and I visited her in New Orleans. God, I had no idea. How did I miss that for so long? How had I carried along in my little bubble with Marcelle while missing that she was slowly driving my friends and family crazy?

All these things, rushing into a second failed marriage, missing the context clues from my friends and family, etc., should have been glaring red flags for me to take a step back from dating and take a step forward into a therapist's office. But that's the thing with emotional pain and uncontrolled anxiety. It's always easier to run and hide and to turn to the salves of booze, women, and late-night New York City parties.

Unfortunately, it would take several more years before I would be ready to confront these demons. And perhaps even more unfortunately, I had to be pushed to my emotional brink in order to finally bury them once and for all.

In reflecting on my marriage with Marcelle, I think my take-away word is "tolerance." She tolerated much more than she deserved. I was not emotionally well when we entered the relationship, and I was even worse off mentally when I left it. But it easily could also be "regret." I regret everything that happened with her. I wish I had been stronger. I wish that I had dealt with my shit appropriately after the first divorce, and I wish that I had never put Marcelle through that whole debacle.

It obviously takes two to tango, and Marcelle rushed in too. Maybe she saw the warning signs with me and ignored them. Maybe she picked up on my anxiety and thought that she could fix me. I'll never know because we never really talked about these kinds of things. That was one of the many reasons the relationship was doomed before we said, "I do." We hadn't established effective lines of communication—about all things but about our feelings in particular—that are requisite to survive the rigors of marriage.

Marcelle wasn't the nicest person I'd ever met, and she likely won't win Miss Congeniality anytime soon. But she deserved a much better outcome than the one she received. Marcelle, if you're reading this, I'd like to say, "I'm sorry."

A Second Pandemic Birthday

For neither good nor evil can last forever; and so it follows that as evil has lasted a long time, good must now be close at hand.

—Miguel de Cervantes

If my dad could see what I'm writing for this book, I think that he would be appalled. Stoic to a fault, the man kept everything to himself until the day that he died. In fact, I learned more about him the day after he died from his estranged brother who finally showed up to bury him than I had ever learned from him while he was alive.

My father was allergic to emotions. I'm sure now, after years of therapy, that he's the one who taught me how to bottle it all up, to soldier on, and to speak nothing of what ails you. All those skills did was to delay the inevitable, to delay the diagnosis, and to permit my path of destruction to carry on for years too long.

The inevitable diagnosis was that I was rampaging through the dating world with undiagnosed and untreated anxiety disorder. This condition made me truly undatable from the standpoint of forming a healthy long-term relationship—a fact that was completely lost on me during the time in which I was rampaging. I was irritable, moody, paranoid, and deeply devoid of self-worth. I had become the quintessential anxious-attachment style, clinging to the first female to show me a modicum of interest. My entire self-worth was externally derived; I was completely terrified of myself and of being alone. Many of these facts are probably not all that surprising to you, dear reader, given what you just learned about my time with Marcelle.

Thinking now, it's hard to identify what would appall my dad more: the fact that I'm having these feelings, or the fact that I'm sharing them. To be fair, he probably had them too. I just never knew it because we never spoke of such things. I wonder if he would condemn me for being this weak, for letting myself degrade so much to be so needy of others, for needing to reach out for help instead of "solving it myself." I think that such a public display of this much interiority would make his skin crawl.

My father was not a callous man, so I know that he would also see some redeeming qualities in me to balance the mental health failures. After all, I had moved to New York, a place he considered an intellectual mecca. And I am writing a book, something that the English major inside of him would certainly love—even if he abhorred the topic. Perhaps he might even be jealous of my career successes, as he was chronically underemployed for a man of his talents.

But would he vocalize these feelings, either positive or negative? Or would he, even if alive, keep a silence that mirrors the one that I am forced to endure by his untimely passing in 2008? As much as I would love to be my eternally optimistic self here, I think that were he still with us, I would receive barely a few muttered words or phrases expressing content or discontent.

This complex relationship with my father certainly impacted my love life. "Words of affirmation" has always been my top love language, both in giving and receiving. I spent my childhood longing for verbal confirmation of my worth, so I naturally seek to give that to my partners, even as I crave it from them.

Nearing the end of 2020, I was not in good shape. After the two failed attempts at finding a mental health provider in the summer of that year, my anxiety had continued to worsen. And while I had brief reprieves from the soul-crushing loneliness of the pandemic—like my dates with Amy and Sasha—my dating life in 2020 had been just a fruitless as in 2019. The cumulative weight of these compounding years of romantic failures was only fueling my anxiety more and driving me to lean into my quixotic quest with even more fervor.

Heading into the first pandemic winter, my pursuit of a partner was becoming frantic. Up until then, the warm summer weather had carried into the fall, which had permitted me to gather with friends outside and mitigate some of the solitude. But with cold weather approaching, I knew that if I didn't find someone fast, I would be condemned to spend the winter quarantining with the cat. As appealing as it sounded to finally have the time to teach her to play the piano, I knew that I had to find a human female to hibernate with.

As fate would have it, my prayers were answered just in time. In November of 2020, I matched with Emma on Hinge. Emma was from England, but she had moved to the States to pursue her career in marketing. After some brief banter on the apps, mostly about COVID-19 precautions and whatnot, we set a date to meet for our first date.

I stood outside the restaurant waiting for Emma, bathed in the crisp autumnal air of a mid-November night. The COVID-19 pandemic had acclimated the residents of New York City to experiencing all major life events while being exposed to the elements, and tonight was no exception. The forecast called for an aggressive rainstorm, and I had prepared accordingly. As I waited anxiously for Emma to arrive, I occupied my busy mind by inspecting the sturdy apparatus that Baby Brasa had erected directly onto Seventh Avenue. With a Plexiglas ceiling and three semipermanent-looking walls, this structure seemed capable of keeping us dry and somewhat warm.

Emma appeared, walking calmly northward toward our outdoor diner. As one does when meeting a semi-blind date in the age of ubiquitous face masks, I squinted to be sure it was her. My confusion was compounded further by her piercing green eyes, which caught me off guard as I was sure hers were brown from studying her blurry Hinge photos. No matter now, she was here, and we ushered to our table to begin our evening.

Straight away, her beauty was striking. In addition to the aforementioned green eyes, she had lovely sandy-blond hair cropped just below her shoulders and a smile that absolutely lit up our three-sided outdoor room. As we shared our first pisco sour and got acquainted, I found myself disarmed by her kind and amiable glow, which immersed me like a warm bath and put my mind immediately at ease. The conversation was flowing effortlessly. She regaled me, in her lyrical English accent, with stories of all her worldly travels and of her past lives in Dubai and South Korea. I in turn shared my own rambling path toward New York City and, feeling quite at home with her, opened up about my own past and my divorce. This didn't seem to faze her in the slightest, which further put my mind at ease.

As we slid in on our second pisco sour, the weather predictably turned. Wind and rain shook our little shack as people scurried and hurried for shelter. The sudden violent cloudburst, quite out of season for mid-November, provided a romantic and surreal backdrop to what was already becoming a special evening. Our conversation had turned to the important stuff—our values, our goals, and our future plans. The evening crested when Emma was explaining to me that she didn't want to have children. She wanted to have a family. What she said resonated so deeply with me that I couldn't take my eyes off her while she said it. It was every bit how she said it as what she said. She was so calm and certain yet so warm and inviting.

Before I knew it, there was a third pisco sour in front of me that my date had seemingly ordered intentionally to prolong the joy of this first rendezvous. We chatted away for another hour or so, until the fated hands on my green wristwatch landed on 10:00 p.m., and the bar closed and asked us to leave. As I walked her home through the hazy remnants of the departing storm, I knew unequivocally that I would seal this date with a kiss. Once we arrived at her front door, I knew the moment was nigh. As our lips met, the last thing my eyes saw before they closed was her hand dropping her umbrella. The kiss was long, slow, and so, so good. As we parted ways and I stumbled away into the dark streets of the sleeping west village, I was completely disoriented. I actually walked in circles for several minutes before righting my course toward the subway.

Sounds so romantic, right? Based off that retelling, I'm sure that you, my dear reader, feel assured that Emma and I rode off into the sunset and lived happily ever after, just as I'd always dreamed; and my quixotic quest would finally be fulfilled.

Not quite. By February of 2021, Emma and I had already had several explosive fights. I went on a ski trip with some friends (I don't ski), just to get out of the town for a weekend and clear my head in the mountains. My friends were gently urging me to reconsider my relationship with Emma, but I was completely crippled by then by my anxiety. The fear of being alone was paralyzing, and even though I knew in my heart of hearts that I was not in the right place, I returned from the trip and reunited with Emma.

Things stabilized upon my return. Emma and I went on a long, cold walk through Central Park and talked about our feelings, our needs, and our boundaries. Well, she talked, that is. At this point in my mental health journey, I was still very much my father's son, and I added little to the conversation in terms of my own wants and needs. The only "need" I could conceive in my head was to preserve the relationship at all costs, to not end up on my own again. I was exhausted of my quixotic quest and could not face the stark reality of Bumble and Hinge any longer. So I kept my mouth shut, listened intently to her wish list, and did my best to dutifully implement it without giving any thought to my own wants or needs.

Heading into the summer, Emma and I were in a good place. My fortieth birthday was approaching, and she had planned a surprise. I was allowed to know that we were going away on a weekend trip together, but the rest of the details were shrouded in secrecy.

Needless to say, I was ecstatic. The stench of my thirty-ninth birthday was still ripe in my nostrils, and I was eager to cleanse my palate with a normal birthday getaway with my girlfriend. Just like all my friends and family, who had long been in stable relationships or marriages, I felt like I had finally joined the idyllic relationship club. I felt like a fully formed human for the first time in a long time.

Emma and I departed the city in the afternoon on June 4, and I drove north. She was my navigator, and I was essentially driving blind. Emma was cleaver enough to disguise our destination by not connecting her phone to the car's navigation, so for the first time in a long time, I was driving based on verbal instructions from my passenger. The nostalgia of this moment was not lost on me, as I think that I was probably in high school the last time I had driven somewhere new without GPS.

We left around ten thirty in the morning, armed with our usual road trip fuel of coffee and almond croissants from Seven Grams Caffé. After just over two hours of driving, we reached our first destination: Upward Brewing Co., which was just north of Liberty, New York. Tucked away in the Catskills, this gem was the perfect ingress for the weekend. Situated back from the main road and nestled in a small clearing among the trees, the main brewery house resembled a grand log cabin mansion. Huge windows flanked the front face of the building, offering a glorious visage of the surrounding nature.

Inside, the decor was delightfully retro, with a distinct mid-century modern flare. The bicolor chairs were all leather, with a deep-golden-brown front juxtaposed with a bright-burgundy back. Aside from the flamboyant chandeliers, the rest of the inside was appropriately spartan, and the nicely muted gray cement floors offered no distraction from the swanky furniture. The beer selection was poignant and simple, with only a few selected items available on tap. Emma was not much of a beer drinker, something that I had long ago forgiven her for, and so she ordered a cider. I ordered a juicy, hazy IPA, and we left the newly acquired comforts of our retro upstate brewery in favor of the firepit outside, which was surrounded by a platoon of Adirondack chairs.

The air outside was immersive and crisp, an unusual treat for early June. As we sipped our drinks out front, I felt a wonderful sense of calm was over me. We had escaped the frenetic city, and we were only a few more minutes away from our eventual destination for the weekend. As the foam lines formed by the bubbles of my IPA slowly drifted downward in my pint glass, I was also starting to feel a sense of accomplishment. Indeed, there were pangs resonating within me that perhaps, on my fortieth birthday, I had finally done it. The quixotic quest was finally competed; Emma was the one. After all, she had planned this amazing getaway and to a brewery no less. She has shucked her own aversion to beer so that I could enjoy something that I love. That's a sure sign of true love, right?

In 1932, Walter B. Pitkin published the American self-help book *Life Begins at Forty*. This book was written during a time of rapid increase in life expectancy, and it hence become quite popular in its time. It was the number one bestselling nonfiction book in the United States in 1933 and number two in 1934, according to *Publishers Weekly*. I actually don't know anything more about the book, having not read it, but somehow the title kept resonating in my head the entire time that Emma and I were upstate celebrating my fortieth birthday. Having survived all the strife and struggle of the last year plus of the pandemic, I was sure that my new life was going to begin at forty, and its genesis would be nestled in the forests and breweries of the Catskill Mountains.

After departing the brewery, we headed east for about fifteen minutes, until we arrived at our birthday weekend oasis. The DeBruce, a mansion-turned-inn, was situated on over six hundred sprawling acres along the Willowemoc Creek. This area is credited with some of the earliest fly-fishing in the United States, a heritage that the DeBruce still effusively espouses on its website.

Upon check-in, we were ushered upstairs to our quarters, which was a quaint (but impeccably decorated) room. I laid in bed while Emma was getting ready, and the fresh early summer air trickled in through a barely open window. The DeBruce staff were alerted that was my birthday, so they had left a bottle of champaign on ice in the corner of our small habitat, which I promptly popped while Emma was getting ready for dinner.

Friday was the fourth, so my birthday was not yet upon us. After an early dinner and exploring the grounds with our dwindling daylight, we settled into bed for an early evening after playing a few rounds of Uno. I had never played before, and Emma had to teach me how to play from scratch. She was kind and let me win a few hands, which allowed us to continue playing for several hours. Almost a year later, when I was finally getting around to throwing away my memorabilia from the DeBruce, I found that scorecard that we kept from our Uno games. Despite everything that had happened in the interlude between those Junes, I still smiled at seeing the scores of lines notched along the page, each indicating not only the evenness of our match but also the closeness that we shared on those special evenings up in the Catskills.

The next day was balmy and beautiful, so we took full advantage. The DeBruce has miles of its own hiking trails, and so we set out around 9:00 a.m. to fully explore the grounds. We each had chosen green as our color by coincidence. Emma was wearing a green tank top, with short jean shorts and a pair of really fetching brown hiking boots. As we descended into the forest, we were surrounded by a canopy of verdant treetops, which filtered the sunlight into a chartreuse sky. Indeed, the visual effects of this distorted sunlight were quite pronounced, as I felt like we were in an immersive green experience. Various shades of hunter, forest, sage, Kelly, and emerald flashed and shone all around use. Emma was walking in front of me, and she almost seemed to blend in, if not completely disappear into this green universe.

The surrealistic nature of this experience has stuck with me until this day. Those canopies in the forests around the DeBruce became a sort of happy place, one I would return to in my mind's eye often in time since my fortieth birthday. On one very impactful evening, I think that I was metaphysically back at the DeBruce, and my past finally caught up with my present self. It was over a year after that weekend in the Catskills, and my yoga studio was hosting a benefit for the war in Ukraine. The main teacher at my studio is of Ukrainian heritage, so he was very passionate about this cause. He had arranged a special class, whereby the entry fee would go to a donation to support the women and children displaced by the violence.

Mitch has always been the most spiritual of the teachers at Sonic Yoga in Hell's Kitchen, and he frequently takes a lot of time in Savasana to guide us in mediation. On this evening in the summer of 2022, he was in rare form. I'm not sure if it was the excitement and emotions surrounding the benefit, but Mitch was determined that evening to press us forward into uncharted spiritual territory.

As Savasana began, Mitch instructed us to close our eyes. "Imagine that you're in a forest," he gently commanded. He went on to describe the forest, with the warm sunlight shining upon our faces and the refreshing breeze spilling over us. A nearby brook babbled and bubbled in the background. The air was calm, and we were at peace.

I almost at once found myself back in the forest of the DeBruce. At that moment, I didn't know why my subconscious mind went there immediately, but I would soon find out. Mitch was now stoking a singing bowl to aid in our meditation, and I found myself falling further into this quasi-hallucinatory experience.

As we fell deeper into the "woods," Mitch suddenly changed the pitch and tone of his voice. "Suddenly," he said, "you become aware that you are not alone. You stand up and look off into the distance of the forest. At first, you cannot make out what you're seeing. Then after, straightening your eyes, you can make out the shape of a figure. Slowly, the figure rounds into form. Who is it?" He inquired, "Who is with you there in the forest?"

I was, of course, staring directly at my deceased father. He was younger than I remembered, perhaps an age that I had only seen him at when I was too young to form meaningful memories. He was staring directly at me, and we shared that gaze for an undetermined period of time. Eventually, he nodded, turned, and walked off into the forest.

It was then that I noticed the singing bowl cease its song, and Mitch was beckoning us back into the yoga studio. The woods of the DeBruce slowly faded from around me, as I drifted from that astral plane back and onto the floor of 944 Eighth Avenue. My eyes shot open as my body was covered with goosebumps, and I realized that I was shivering and sweating simultaneously. After the shock of the moment receded, I reflected on the beauty of what had just transpired. That meeting with my father was one of the many beautiful healing experiences that defined the summer of 2022.

Back to the summer of 2021, Emma and I finished our hike around noon and returned to the DeBruce to lounge by the pool before dinner. The sun was now quite hot, and the chilly pool water offered a nice reprieve from the heat. After we were both appropriately sun-kissed, we went back to the room to shower before dinner.

The dining room itself was a sight to behold. It was glassed walled on all sides and perched on the corner of the lodge overlooking the mountain and the valley. As it was summer, they had opened the glass walls, which created an open-air suspended dining experience, the likes of which I'd never seen.

The DeBruce has a world-renowned cuisine, and the night of June 5 was no exception. We ordered the eight-course tasting menu and enjoyed the best, most scrumptious Michelin-quality meal that I've ever eaten.

After dinner, we sat outside by one of the firepits near the back of the estate. We were completely immersed in nature, with only the dim lights emitted by the DeBruce itself to break of the monopoly of the dark night around us. Under a blanket of twinkling stars, we closed out my birthday redemption. On the drive back to the city the next day, I can remember thinking to myself that if life truly began at forty, then I was at the start of what would surely be a wonderful life with Emma.

Epilogue

As you, my gentle reader, are no doubt astute to my foreshadowing, you know that my fortieth birthday was not the start of life happily ever after. Far from it, unfortunately.

By the fall of 2021, Emma and I were in a free fall. What was a very unimportant argument in September of that year was escalated into a giant fight that forever broke the relationship. Emma went nuclear with this one, even going so far as to cancel her ticket to come with me to a conference in Denver. We had tickets to see a concert at the Red River Amphitheater, which I had always wanted to visit, but she canceled anyway. I didn't go to the concert, but I still had to go on the trip without her, as it was for work.

When I returned, Emma had fully retreated into herself. What I know now that I didn't really appreciate then was that Emma was still dealing with a lot of unresolved childhood trauma, which not only prevented her from expressing vulnerability with partners, but it made her very sensitive to other people's anger. I had lost my temper with her during this fight, and even though I had apologized, she had already completely shut down and withdrawn.

The months that followed were dark. Emma and I would see each other a few nights per week, but despite this perfunctory time spent physically with each other, the emotional gulf between us was enormous. I was completely despondent, as I was not capable of standing on my own emotionally. Prior to the fight, Emma had become a safe harbor, and with her gone emotionally, I was lost in a sea of despair. Pushed to this breaking point and completely riddled with anxiety, I finally reached out for help again.

This time, my search was more successful. Through an app, I was able to find a good therapist in Buffalo. One of the perks of the post-pandemic world, I suppose, was that therapy could now be completed entirely online, and the fact that my therapist was eight hours away was not an issue.

I spent the rest of 2021 meeting with my therapist once a week. She introduced me to schema therapy, and while I felt that I was gaining a better understanding of some of the reasons that I was so anxious, I wasn't actually feeling less anxious. Throughout the early days of schema therapy, I was introduced to the modes: child modes, coping modes, parent modes, and the healthy adult mode. The latter was obviously the desired end product of therapy, whereas the former (angry child mode, in particular) was where most people started. I became interested in happy child mode, and I found this idea of nurturing out most basic desires from childhood especially appealing.

I thought about the last time that I was really in happy child mode. Going back to my earliest childhood memories, I reflected on the cartoons and shows that I had watched with my dad. He was a geek about these shows, and he would buy me all the action figures: *He-Man*, *ThunderCats*, *G.I. Joe*, you name it. If it was a popular early eighties kids television show, then my dad and I were probably into it.

So on those long, lonely nights in the second winter of the pandemic, when my partner was effectively ignoring me, the cat and I were holed up in my apartment watching remakes of all the classics. As fate would have it, there was a fairly recent remake of the original *Masters of the Universe* that was playing as a series on Netflix.

After watching this series and several others like it, I finally did start to feel less anxious. In therapy, I had learned that one of my other schemas is unrelenting standards, which was undoubtedly something that I had inherited from both Mom and Dad. These unrelenting standards drove me to success in my career, as I was completely tenacious in my pursuit of success and recognition. However, these unrelenting standards also prohibited me from ever relaxing. Indeed, once I started pharmacy school, all the shenanigans ceased. Video games, cartoons (I was into anime at the time), etc., were all excised from my life to make time for school and pharmacy. I was actually still in a backyard wrestling league with my high school friends up until age twenty-one, when I entered pharmacy school. Sadly, that favorite childhood pastime also fell by the wayside.

So to finally relent my unrelenting standards and permit myself to watch cartoons was a really big deal—a first step, one of many eventual steps, toward finally finding true inner peace.

Emma and I were still together at New Years somehow, but things were steadily deteriorating. We had another massive fight around Valentine's Day. This one was even more insignificant than the one in September, as we were fighting over Instagram of all things. After that fight, she said she was ready to break up, and I was happy to oblige. We parted ways, only to find out about four days later that Emma had just had a miscarriage.

It had started out like any other period, but it was harder and more consistent. Eventually becoming ceaseless, she went to the doctor, only to find out that she had been pregnant and had lost the embryo. We were definitely not trying to have kids, and the bitter irony of us getting pregnant the last time we had sex was not lost on me. Especially given our respective ages, I think that we were both surprised with how easily we had conceived.

While we were both upset, she was more devastated than I. This tragedy could not have been more poorly timed. Just as we were trying to distance ourselves from each other, fate forced us back together for another few agonizing months. We were two broken people trying to support each other through a terrible tragedy, which was like laying tragedies on top of one another. Indeed, the situation in that winter of 2022 was a seven-layer shit cake.

Emma and I were both emotionally spent from the long months of war with each other, which had been vacillating between cold and hot. I truly wanted to get away from the relationship, but I think that it was my guilt that kept me there, even though I knew deep down that I was a lousy support system in my current condition. I spent a lot of my own time in therapy talking about Emma's feelings, which wasn't helping me to get better or to deal with my own emotions.

Emma was bedridden, inconsolable at times, and racked by fits of melancholy. In these moments, while I was trying to be closest to her, I could only feel the space between us widening. I was very sad about the loss of the baby, for I have always wanted to be a father, and I know that no matter how bad things were between us, I would have been a good parent to that child.

But I feel that my grief was blunted by a sense of relief that we hadn't ended up bringing a child into our fucked-up little universe. At that point, I had given up hope that the relationship was salvageable; and so while I, too, was grief-stricken, a small part of me kept thinking that we might have dodged a bullet.

Mercifully, in April, Emma and I finally called it quits. I left for Boston on a work trip right after it happened; and after spending a week basically living the life of a local on the Back Bay, I returned home to New York and promptly caught COVID-19. The ensuring week of quarantine provided me with additional space to process the shock and the hurt of losing both the unborn child and the person whom I had once thought was the end of my quixotic quest. The sickness was a blessing in disguise, for at least a week, I wasn't able to even begin to ask myself, "What's next?" in terms of dating, seeing as how I was forbidden from being around other people. If there's one thing that can halt a quixotic quest, it's a highly contagious virus.

It was then that I made a fateful decision that would alter the rest of 2022 and, likely, the rest of my life. While in quarantine, I called up my therapist and requested to finally start on an antidepressant medication. In my quarantine, I had been reading books on anxiety, and one on neuroplasticity really spoke to me. For those who are unfamiliar, here's a handy description from our old pal, ChatGPT:

> Neuroplasticity refers to the brain's ability to change and reorganize itself throughout an individual's life. It is the ability of the brain to form new neural connections and pathways in response to new experiences, learning, or changes in the environment.
>
> Neuroplasticity occurs in various forms, such as structural changes in the brain's neurons, changes in the strength and efficiency of synaptic connections between neurons, and changes in the overall organization of brain networks. It is a fundamental process underlying learning, memory, and recovery from injury or disease.
>
> Neuroplasticity research has shown that the brain can adapt and change in response to environmental factors, such as physical exercise, cognitive training, meditation, and exposure to new experiences. It also plays a critical role in the development of new treatments for neurological and psychiatric disorders, such as stroke, traumatic brain injury, depression, and **anxiety**.

Bingo. The idea of being able to rewire my anxious brain with the help of therapy and pharmaceuticals was too tempting to pass up. My therapist happily agreed, and I started on a low dose of an SSRI (selective serotonin reuptake inhibitor) before I exited quarantine.

And the rest, they say, dear reader, was history.

A Gentleman's Journey Home

It's up to brave hearts, sir, to be patient when things are going badly, as well as being happy when things are going well.

—Miguel de Cervantes

Everyone that has Instagram, Facebook, or TikTok no doubt has their favorite videos. And everyone who has these apps also knows that the apps know what your favorite videos and topics are. The "secret sauce" with respect to these companies is their algorithms, which curate your viewing based on its deductive prowess and your past search histories. One of my favorite videos was served up to me just in this manner, no doubt selected by the bot based on its assessment of my predictions and peculiarities.

At the peak of the pandemic, I was probably consuming the same excessive-level screen time with these apps as everyone else. Indeed, I was slowly going stir crazy in my feline-dominated quarantine, having no bipedal roommates to converse with or dominate in Monopoly. Hence, I started taking random pictures and videos of the cat and posting them on my personal Instagram account under the moniker of Covid Kitty.

In addition to boosting the morale of the tens and tens of people who follow me on Instagram, Covid Kitty was actually performing a public health service. Each Covid Kitty video was accompanied by either a public health or mental health message. Below are just a few of my favorites of the nearly daily updates that Covid Kitty provided.

Upon using her scratching post, she snapped a pic and captioned, "Covid Kitty says stay indoors and scratch that itch with some alone time!" It helped that her eggplant toy was in the picture as well.

Upon finishing up with licking her paws, she snapped a picture and said, "Covid Kitty has excellent paw hygiene. Be like Covid Kitty and wash your paws!"

Upon completing a quick yoga sesh, she snapped a video and said, "Covid Kitty stays fit doing yoga at home. Be like Covid Kitty and stay fit during quarantine!"

I know, solid gold, right? While I gained exactly zero new followers as a result of the Covid Kitty takeover of my social media, I did entertain myself thoroughly. Most of my closest friends still refer to her as Covid Kitty, and she responds to "Kitty" more than to her actual name.

Anyway, back to my favorite video! This gem is definitely in my top ten, and when I tell you what it was about, you may be surprised to learn that it was selected by the algorithm for my viewing pleasure. I'm aware that up to this point in the book, I've mostly (emphasis on mostly) presented myself as a middle-aged gentleman, stoic college professor, and serious about my quixotic quest for true love. However, I also have fifth-grade sense of humor. Poop jokes, in particular, are my weakness. And while I also love a good dad joke—as I am now old enough to properly appreciate them—I love a good poop joke. So now with that preface, on to this video.

It's a clip of someone's Ring doorbell camera. The caption from the poster says, "The guy I hooked up with last night," and as the video starts, the camera is facing out over a cold and barren snowscape. So immediately without any characters, I identify with this video, as it looks like somewhere in the Midwest, where I grew up. As the video proceeds, a fat dude in his thirties stumbles out from the door, adorned in flannel and a floppy winter hat that loosely covers his ears.

At this point, I'm now positive that this is from the Midwest, as this guy looks like he walked out a bar in Northern Michigan or Wisconsin and into this girl's home after a night of heavy drinking at the local watering hole. But what happens next, well that, my gentle readers, *is* pure gold.

This guy proceeds to let out a ten-second fart, one that he had no doubt been holding all morning after waking up next his hookup from the night prior. This fart was loud, violent, and persistent; and upon hearing it, I was immediately concerned about the condition of this poor guy's trousers. But the kicker was the first comment left below the video: "a true gentleman."

I was dead upon seeing this. To be fair, the commenter had a point. After all, based on the caption of the poster, this guy was just some one-night stand that she had picked up the night before. Who was he to struggle against Mother Nature to suppress his early morning God-given gaseous expulsions for just some girl that he convinced to sleep with him? Yet in spite of their relative unfamiliarity, this flatulent saint held it together until he was outside. Once I finished laughing, I found myself slightly admiring this gassy gentleman. Yet, little did I know then that his intestinal fortitude would serve as inspiration to me in my own flatus-related misadventure.

The days that followed my breakup with Emma were quite unpleasant. Having COVID-19 while going through a breakup is not a combo I would wish on anyone. What happened next, however, was completely transformative. Despite being in therapy since the fall and spending evenings nurturing my inner child by debating with the cat whether *He-Man* or *ThunderCats* was the better Saturday morning eighties cartoon, I was still not really progressing. No matter how hard I tried with my therapist, the intervals in between visits were still racked with anxiety. The fear of dying a lonely, flatulent old man was pervasive, and the constant thought stream of negative self-talk was impossible to silence.

Until the SSRI. I started to feel calmer within a few weeks of starting the medication. The endless loop of negative self-talk, unrelenting standards, abandonment schemas, etc., all ceased. My head was quiet. My thoughts were clear. I felt a peace that I had not felt in years, one that had perhaps eluded me for my entire life in New York.

Things really took off after that. Removing the constant negative white noise from my background allowed me to really be present in therapy. The breakthroughs really started happening almost every week. I started to journal in a Google doc with my therapist in order to keep up with the insights that I cleaned from revisiting my past and present circumstances with a clear head. I was able to understand how my complicated relationship with my parents (my father in particular) had shaped my unhealthy views on relationships.

Separating from Emma was like removing a troublesome splinter that had prevented a wound from healing properly. The relationship had deteriorated so much that it was introducing cognitive dissonance. For every step forward I took with therapy, the pain and strife of the relationship took it back. But with that in the past, I was finally able to focus on myself fully and work toward the root of what was really troubling me.

My approach to healing was holistic. In addition to locking into therapy every week, I put my butt into the yoga studio at least five nights a week. I also read voraciously, consuming books on mental health, anxïety, and on the human condition at-large. One book above the rest dominated my summer of 2022. Indeed, I would spend at least one afternoon every weekend curled up under a tree in Central Park reading this book. This particular book I read slowly, deliberately, because the information was too important to pass through quickly.

That book was *Atlas of the Heart* by Brené Brown. The premise of the book is that we cannot even begin to understand and express our emotions effectively if we lack the adequate definitions for our own emotions. So in this anthology, Dr. Brown delves painstakingly through every emotion, delivering exhaustive research while simultaneously personifying the language of human emotion. For anyone looking to enhance their understanding of the human experience and what it means to feel, well, anything, I would highly recommend this book.

Of all the interventions that I enacted in the summer of 2022, the most crucial was the postponement of my quixotic quest. I did keep my dating profiles active, but my target audience was no longer my forever person. So while I did date casually through those early spring into summer months of 2022, I was not pressuring myself with the enormity of finding a life partner.

Part of how I had always sabotaged my mental health was by trapping my consciousness in the future, always obsessing about the next agenda item, the next to-do-list task, and—in the case of my quest—the next first date. Indeed, I look back now with some remorse at all the happy moments that I was not fully present. Weddings, in particular, of very dear friends, are some of the worse examples of this preoccupation. I was usually off by myself, moping and feeling anxious for having not found my own life partner, rather than reveling with everyone else and being happy for my loved ones. Only now, in a state of well-being, can I see how tragic that behavior was.

So in the summer of 2022, all that stopped because I literally stopped. When I was at the park, there were afternoons where I wouldn't read much, instead preferring to just lounge under the tree and stare at the sky or get lost in watching squirrels chase each other. Before the new medication, this kind of behavior would have been impossible. My old self would never permit such a "waste of time," as a leisurely siesta in Central Park.

It was in these moments of solitude that I found my emotional solemnity and finally freed myself from the intoxicating and ceaseless pursuit of a quest. And then something fascinating happened. Once I finally got out from underneath the weight of my quest, I was actually able to understand what it truly was.

Through the therapy, the medication, the yoga, the books, and the peace in the park, I was at last able to see that my quest was always about love but not the love that I thought I was chasing all along. I had thought that the quest began when I moved to New York, but through many sessions with my therapist, I was able to see that the actually began in childhood. The quixotic quest to find true love was not actually a quest to find my forever person.

The ache in my heart—that void of love that I was seeking to fill and which I had mistaken as a void of martial love—was actually a void of self-love. Even as a child, I was projecting this void onto others when I would see an adult without a wedding ring and immediately start to pity them and imagine them alone in their sad little life. I could never understand why I always did that—all the way into adulthood—until the therapy of the summer of 2022. I was projecting my own sadness and grief onto them. It was my void that I was seeing, just as a manifestation as someone else's imaginary suffering.

What a mind fuck this revelation was. This quest, which had dominated my consciousness for so long, was never about true love in the sense of a finding a romantic partner. In the summer of 2022, I finally discovered that it was self-love that I was subconsciously chasing all along.

This revelation, which was one of many during that summer, was utterly freeing. And it only supported my initial instincts back in the fall of 2021, when I started to look inward for happiness as my relationship with Emma was crumbling. "To thine own self be true" might as well be the slogan for this book. To only find out in my early forties that I had not been true to myself for a long time was a bit disheartening at first, but the relief that I felt from finally understanding the quest brought me the deepest peace that I've ever felt in my life.

The rest of the summer of 2022 was nurturing and relaxing. Although I had been casually seeing a few people here and there, as the leaves began to turn colors and the predictable autumnal chill crept over New York, I started to feel the itch to start dating a little more deliberately again. Fortunately, my trusty dating companion—the Internet—was ready to oblige me.

So I dusted off my Bumble and Hinge accounts, lathered them up with loads of pop psych catchphrases like "I've done the hard work," and cast my net. This time, however, I had a surprise beset me from left field.

I love Instagram for its endless supply of solid-gold feline content, but Instagram can also absolutely be used as a dating tool. How this is usually accomplished is through sliding into someone's direct messages, or DMs.

Now I realize that some of you are familiar with this topic while other readers may not be. So I'll elaborate by asking our trusty sidekick, ChatGPT, to define the DM slide:

> To "slide into someone's DMs" is a colloquial expression that refers to sending a direct message (DM) to someone on social media, particularly on platforms such as Instagram, Twitter, or Facebook, with the intention of starting a conversation or expressing interest in them romantically or platonically.

And that, my dear reader, is exactly what happened to me in October of 2022. I posted a picture of some dish that I had baked over one of my solitary weekends, and one of the new nurses at the hospital slid into my DMs.

Her question was innocuous, of course. I think that my post must have been football related because she responded simply asking if my team won. But that innocent little introduction spurred a long text thread that eventually led to us planning our first date over drinks later that week.

Standing at least my height, with piercing blue eyes and long blond hair, Ivanna stood out immediately from any crowd. She had a very athletic build and clearly seemed dedicated to physical fitness. Based on her Instagram photos, she also appeared to have children, which made her attention to her fitness even more impressive, given how much time it takes to raise children as a single mom.

The beauty of using Instagram for the purpose of dating is that one has access to a large repository of photos, which offers a much wider visage of a potential partner's life compared to the limited data presented on most dating apps. In scrolling through Ivanna's pictures, I gleaned that she was either active military or had served previously, and she was currently in school pursuing her master's degree in nursing.

Combining these things together, I realized that at least on paper, Ivanna was a great candidate for life-partner status. However,

I was not rushing forward toward any forgone conclusions. While I was dabbing my toe back into the dating scene, I was not yet formally resuming my quixotic quest. "Take it slow," I can remember telling myself. "Just enjoy the ride."

Ivanna and I set to meet after work for drinks. She lived not far from my work, so it was easy enough to find a spot near downtown Brooklyn. I was early, of course, and as our date was at 5:00 p.m. or 5:30 p.m., there were few other patrons at the bar when Ivanna arrived.

Ivanna was very beautiful in person, but it was her physical presence that really made an immediate impact. The way that she carried herself was so poised, so self-assured. She was not overly talkative, but she was absolutely engaging and very funny. I wasn't so surprised by her sense of humor, as I had been following her Instagram for a while, and she was always posting funny stuff. And while English was not her first language, she was fluent in dad jokes, and her comedic timing was perfect.

I had a hunch that Ivanna was foreign-born and that was confirmed by her heavy accent. While I thought that she might be Russian, I later learned that she was Ukrainian, and she had moved to the US when she was a teenager with her parents. Like most kids who immigrate, she had to work twice as hard for everything, and Ivanna had worked very hard to get to where was currently. She had in fact served in the military, as she had to enlisted in the Army to pay for her nursing school after her first divorce.

Yes, that's right, Ivanna was twice divorced, just like yours truly. Needless to say, I felt an immediate connection to her when I learned of this. And she did have children, two actually, one from each ex-husband.

So despite the cultural differences, we seemed more similar than different. I was so pleasantly surprised by this person that I could scarcely believe it. I wasn't necessarily expecting much from someone who had randomly slid into my DMs, but instead, I met this very funny person with a deep sense of work ethic and a strong commitment to family, all traits that were music to my Midwestern ears.

We eventually left the bar and found a local seafood place, as Ivanna is a pescatarian. After dinner, I drove her home; and while parked in front of her apartment, she told me that she would love to invite me up for a nightcap. But her daughter was with her that week, and she would prefer we wait until next week when she would be with her father. I was a little taken aback by her directness, but at the same time, I loved her honesty. As I drove home, I was already excited for our second date.

Nearly a week later, I was drudging through another long Thursday at my Brooklyn office. In addition to being a pharmacist at the hospital, I also split my time teaching at a college of pharmacy, and Thursday was my usual day to be on campus. I had recently agreed to take on a two-year stint as department chair, so on this particular balmy October Thursday, I was slogging through an enthralling stack of paperwork. As I wrapped up my last batch of grade-change-approval forms, I was packing up my bag to leave when my phone buzzed with a text message from Ivanna.

She was apparently struggling with an assignment in her master's program, and given our intersecting careers in health care, she was imploring for my assistance. In exchange for my services, she was offering to pay me with a nice home-cooked dinner.

Given that my plans for the evening prior to her text had revolved around trying to drug the cat so that I could brush her teeth, this new option presented a significant upgrade. I shot up from my chair and immediately abandoned the rest of my chair responsibilities for the day.

I didn't realize that I didn't know where I was going until I was already in my car, and upon finding out that she lived quite near campus and wasn't ready for me until 6:00 p.m., I had some time to kill. So I stopped by the local watering hole across the street from campus. Most of the patrons were older people who, at least based on my overhearing of their stories, had been in the neighborhood for quite some time. The place was poorly lit, the decor was very seventies, and the stool that I perched upon had definitely had at least ten thousand other asses on it during its illustrious career. The stool was encased in sandy-brown leather that was cracked and worn, so much so that when I shifted my weight from one cheek to the next, I worried that these tiny leather fingernails would fray my work trousers.

The drink menu was simple, so I ordered my favorite—a gin and tonic with lime. While a simple concoction, I enjoy not only the drink but also its history. As the lore goes, British sailors in the nineteenth century were afforded rations of gin to prevent mutiny, limes to prevent survey, and quinine (in the form of tonic) to fight malaria. All these ingredients are unpalatable on their own, so one ingenious sailor eventually decided to combine all three and in doing so created one of the world's most popular drinks. Neat, huh?

Anyway, I slowly sipped my G and T and steeled my nerves for what was to come. I was intimidated by Ivanna for many reasons. She was an accomplished clinician, an Army veteran, an aspiring student, and—most importantly—a mother of two. Of all her accolades, I think that one deserves the most respect. I treat all my dates respectfully, but single moms are in a different class. She is already doing a hero's work in supporting her family and still finding time to go out with a normal guy like me, so the least that she deserves is my upmost reverence and attention.

After finishing my drink, I make the short trip the rest of the way to her apartment. She greets me at the door in pink pajama bottoms and a white tank top. While she obviously looked great and even her evening wear was designer, what I loved more was how down-to-earth she was in this moment. This was only our second date, and while she was clearly someone who was very attentive about her looks, she was showing me a casual side and showing me that she had a lot of confidence in herself and who she was naturally.

Despite her distracting attire, we were able to get some of her homework done, until we both started getting hungry. Rather than break from the work, she offered to order in some nosh so that we could finish the assignment. Given her dietary restrictions and our shared love of spicy food, we settled on a large order of Thai food. This decision would, unfortunately, come back to bite me in the ass (literally) later in this date.

After having dinner and finishing what she considered an acceptable amount of homework, she suggested that we retire to her bedroom to watch some old episodes of *Modern Family. What a great choice*, I thought. Throughout our brief time together, her sense of humor continued to surprise me in how similar it was to mine.

On one of our later dates, I finally clarified her long-term career aspirations. She wanted to finish her nurse practitioner degree so that she could one day open her own clinic providing a wide range of cosmetic procedures, like Botox injections, liquid rhinoplasty, and lip fillers. She told me how she had some of these procedures before and how instrumental they were in boosting her self-confidence after her divorces. While she wasn't curing cancer with this plan, I still respected and admired her drive to help people and to give back to society in a way that matched up with her personal hopes and dreams.

About thirty minutes or so into the first episode, we started getting handsy. The sex was surprisingly good for a first time with someone new, and afterward, we laid in bed motionless and speechless for quite some time. I had practiced this skill numerous times over the summer, the simple act of being present in the moment and enjoying the feelings I was having rather than rushing on to the next topic or the next activity. *What a great evening*, I thought to myself. Certainly better than watching *Love Is Blind* and reviewing the cat's algebra homework, which is what would have likely occurred after she had outwitted me trying to brush her teeth. Eventually, Ivanna cuddled up next to me, and we fell asleep.

Ivanna had an intense fitness routine, so her alarm went off at 5:30 a.m. Seeing as I was not planning on a sleepover that night and I had not packed my sleeping pills, I was sadly already awake before her alarm went off. Before I could even move, Ivanna leaped deftly out of bed and pranced into the kitchen to make coffee.

I followed sleepily into the kitchen, searching for my shirt and pants along the way. The smell of the coffee was intoxicating; however, I knew that I could not partake. I, like most humans, am gastronomically sensitive to coffee; and being the gentleman that I am, I did not want to blow up this lovely young lady's bathroom on my way out after our first night of being intimate.

Before my eyes were fully open, she turned quickly and offered me a piping hot cup of delicious bean water. In a daze, I shrieked out, "No!" Immediately aware that I had just shrieked for no reason, I regrouped and said, "Um, no, thank you. I don't drink coffee."

A bold-faced lie that was farcical on its face, she twisted her left eyebrow upward as she digested my bizarre admonishment of the bean water. It pained me deeply, both the lie and the refusal of the coffee, for I do so desperately love coffee. But I had to stay strong in refusing the coffee, unless I wanted to end up like the guy in the Ring doorbell video, sharting my way back to Manhattan.

She eventually accepted my excuse for turning down the coffee and walked me down to her parking garage, where I had illegally parked in her neighbor's spot. Relieved to not see a boot on my front tire, I started the car, did a sixteen-point turn, and escaped from the tiny parking prison unscathed and woefully undercaffeinated.

It was dark when I started my journey back, and although I could not see much in the night sky, I was floating on cloud nine. This girl seemed incredible, and while it was only two dates, things were happening so easily. I pondered the old days and my obsession with the quixotic quest and wondered if my obsession with the pursuit had actually blocked me from getting what I wanted in the past. In this instance, it did seem that by stepping out of my own way and letting things happen naturally was paying off.

As I finished the Brooklyn part of my trek home and approached the Hugh L. Carey Tunnel, the sun was starting to peak over the horizon, and I could see the skyline of Manhattan starting to glisten in the fresh morning light. *What a time to be alive*, I thought to myself as I basked in the glory of my triumphant evening.

When I emerged from the tunnel, things had changed drastically. For you see, dear reader, when I was about halfway through the tunnel, the entire Thai food entrée that I had enjoyed the evening prior was now urgently demanding an exodus.

I was now engaged in a life-or-death struggle against the clock. I was immediately drenched in sweat, as every sphincter in my body simultaneously constricted; and my vison blurred, as I focused my entire energy on not shitting my pants. *This will be the end of this car*, I thought to myself. The smell of this Thai food disaster will never come out, and I'll just have to sell the car or burn it in an abandoned parking lot for the insurance money.

The tempo of my drive home accelerated appropriately, and I was now doing twenty over the speed limit up the West Side Highway. This was a white-knuckle drive for the rest of my gentlemanly journey back home. At this point, I was questioning my decision to not use Ivanna's bathroom and started pondering if I should start carrying a small bottle of Poo-Pourri in my workbag for future endeavors like this night out.

After I Tokyo-drifted into my parking garage, I burst into the apartment and scared the living hell out of the cat—who was quietly waiting by the door, arms folded, to judge me for not coming home in time to have her petite déjeuner prepared before sunrise. It was truly a photo finish as I barely made it to the bathroom. Aside from being grateful that I hadn't destroyed my car, I remember feeling betrayed by my body, as a wonderful morning was turned upside down by my slowly aging physiology.

Epilogue

Ivanna is a wonderful person—accomplished, sweet, attractive, driven, and funny. Like I said earlier, on paper, she ticked many boxes. In practice, however, things were less than smooth.

Time was really the major barrier. Ivanna was working full time, in school full time, supporting her daughter, and was still required to periodically contribute time to the Army. This left scant few hours per week for relationships, and after about three weeks of dating, it was clear to me that she and I were not in the same phase of our lives. Despite my postponement of my quest, I was still interested in eventually getting serious with someone. Ivanna was a great person, but she had her hands full with her own life, so I eventually broke things off in late October of 2022.

While things didn't work out with Ivanna, the relationship was nonetheless very refreshing. It was nice to just be with someone without the constant pressure of the quest weighing on me. I really enjoyed just being present with her in the moments that we did have time to spend together. I wasn't especially looking to date when Ivanna slid into my DMs, but I did enjoy going along with it once it happened.

I could sense a huge difference between my "new" self in this relationship versus the other version of me that was wrought with anxiety and motivated by fear of being alone rather than by a true pursuit of love. And while my relationship with Ivanna was relatively brief, it was impactful, as I felt afterward that I had passed my first test of being with someone after my summer of self-work and that I was ready to date more seriously after taking more than six months off to focus on my recovery.

And while I will say that the feelings of inner peace and tranquility that I felt in the relationship were certainly proof that I was ready to resume my quest, the way that second date ended was also a barometer of where I was in my adult life. Almost shitting my pants on the way home, even when I skipped the coffee, was yet another example of how the physiology of forties does not really cooperate with the rigors of dating casually like a twentysomething-year-old.

When I reflected on this latest bodily debacle, I started to add up everything that had happened over the last few years as I aged. While some of the incidences—like the broken finger and the boat shoes— were unlikely to happen again, many of these issues were ongoing. Indeed, when you add weak bowels to unpredictable allergy attacks, chronic insomnia, and an old man back, suddenly, middle-aged dating was looking like a minefield of potential physiological failures.

Therefore, with my mind and spirit healed while my body was slowly decaying, I made up my mind that it was time to resume the quixotic quest. My change in perspective on this go-around was profound, to say the least. In my past quest, I thought all the while that I was chasing something in my pursuit of true love. In reality, I wasn't chasing anything. I was really just running—running from my past, from my fears, and from my self-doubt. So while at first I thought I was "resuming" my quest, in reality, I was just starting it honestly for the first time.

And so, just like the illustrious old knight Don Quixote de La Mancha himself, I donned my shield, located my lance, and mounted my trusty steed.

Which is to say I fired up Bumble and Hinge, updated my six-month-old pictures, and juiced up my bio with all my newly acquired pop psych lingo. I put in my attachment style, my enneagram, and name-dropped Brené Brown more than once. I espoused virtues of vulnerability, openness, and empathy. And of course, I left all my prior spiels about marriage, children, happy home with a white picket fence, etc. In other words, I wrote what I considered to be the perfect profile. *Absolutely irresistible to any reasonable middle-aged women in New York City*, I remember thinking.

Oh yeah, I thought to myself. *This time, it's gonna be different.*

When the Cat Learns German (Die Katze lernt Deutsch)

The heart that loves is always young.

—a random fortune cookie I opened on March 8, 2019

"*Meine Fresse,*" I muttered under my breath, as I was jolted from my slumber and returned from my German-speaking inner world to the English-speaking outer world. What the hell was that sound?

I quickly realized the sound was extremely loud snoring, and it was coming from the guy sleeping next to me. This was our first night sleeping together, and this, I was not prepared for.

Despite growing up in Germany, I had spent a lot of time in the United States. I studied English all through secondary school and spent a year of high school with a host family in Kentucky. Since then, I have been a frequent tourist, often going on long road trips in search of various Hard Rock Café locations all over the country. My usual travel companion for these trips is my mother, who—like this guy—snores like a chainsaw.

My mom's snoring is so pronounced that I had custom earplugs made, which molded to the shape of my ear and effectively blocked out the auditory assaults from her sawing logs at the decibel level of a

Boeing 777. On this particular evening, with this guy doing a similar impression of a jet engine, my earplugs were sorely missed.

I found myself a little annoyed that he hadn't warned me about this, given that I'm sure it was not possible that he didn't know he snored like this. He tended to talk a lot about his exes—too much, at times, if I'm being honest. Surely, they must have told him that he snores like an Ice Road Trucker.

I tried nudging him to get him to turn over, but this was completely ineffective. I laid there for a few futile minutes, and after it became apparent that my eardrums would rupture before I'd fall back to sleep, I got up to go into the living room.

The apartment was dark, and this was my first time at his place, so I had to fumble around for a few minutes to find a light switch. Upon flicking on the kitchen lights, the apartment was suddenly bathed in the soft florescent glow of two long tube light bulbs.

It was then, after the light came on, that I could see this cat sitting directly in the middle of the living room staring at me.

"Ach, *meine Fresse!*" I yelled out.

I immediately threw my hands over my mouth, as if doing so would somehow erase the yelp I had just emitted at being startled by this obese feline. The cat was completely unbothered, and she just continued to stare at me as she awaited my next move.

I had only met this cat a few hours earlier, but she seemed friendly enough. Having not ever had one as a pet, I was a little unsure of how to proceed. I decided that the best course of action was to shuffle around her and settle down in the chair by the window.

After sitting in the chair for a few minutes (I later learned that I had chosen the cat's chair to sit in), she came over and gave my feet a good sniff. After she'd had a nose-full, she seemed to decide that I wasn't an apex predator, and she jumped onto my lap.

I wasn't quite sure what to do next, so I just started petting the cat, hoping that she wouldn't turn feral and take a chunk out of my hand like the cats I see on my Instagram feed. Eventually, she just settled down next to me, and she actually started purring after I was petting her for a while.

At this point, however, I wasn't sure what my next move was. I had left my phone on the nightstand in the bedroom, and I was now pinned down in this chair by this behemoth of a cat. Just then, I noticed that the shelf next to me was full of vinyl records.

This guy and I had not really talked about music at this point, so I was immensely curious to see what he liked enough to get in a 45. Immediately, I noticed that he must like classical music, as nearly every record was something by Beethoven or Mozart. And then I noticed a record by Gustav Mahler, and the title was completely in German! I immediately grabbed it, only then to almost drop it when I saw the title.

"*Kindertotenlider?*" Songs of dead children? What the hell kind of music is this guy into?

Still, I was bored and now pinned down with *die Katze* on my lap, so I flipped over the cover and noticed there were lyrics printed on the back. For no reason at all, really, I started reading aloud to the cat:

> *Nun seh' ich wohl, warum so dunkel Flammen*
> *Ihr spruhtet mir in manchem Augenblicke, O Augen!*
> *Gleichsam um voll in einem Blicke*
> *Zu drangen eure ganze Macht zusammen*
> *Doch ahnt' ich nicht, weil Nebel mich umschwammen*

The cat listened very intently to my reading, so much so that I was convinced that she must be a German cat. *Was eine gut Katze*, I thought as I continued to pet her. After a while of reading and petting, I actually felt rather relaxed, even to the point that I could attempt to sleep again. I gently stood up, and the cat leaped off my lap and ran under the couch. "*Gut schlafen*," I whispered under my breath as I slid back into the bedroom. Mercifully, the Ice Road Trucker had cooled his jets while I was giving the cat her first German lesson, and within a few minutes of climbing back into bed, I was finally fast asleep again.

*****

My initial lurch back into the dating foray was rather unceremonious. Indeed, much like my misaligned literary inspiration, Don Quixote, my launch was beset by a series of failures and setbacks.

My new profile was certainly not to blame, for I was getting a lot of attention from potential suitors. All my new pop psych buzzwords were drawing a lot of matches, and I getting first dates was no problem at all. Unfortunately, I wasn't getting any second dates.

In fact, I had never had such a bad run of dating in my life before. I think that I went on six or seven dud dates in a two-week span. There was Tina, the Sri Lankan oil importer who was generally uninterested from the start of the date; and then Suzy, the businesswoman who insisted that we meet for tea instead of drinks and proceeded to talk about manga for two straight hours before abruptly leaving to go home to "feed her cat." At least she was a fellow animal lover.

And then there was Laura, who, like many of the others, seemed generally uninterested from fairly early in the date. Sensing her energy and feeling quite bored myself with her lack of enthusiasm, I decided to have a little fun. Despite her generally flat affect, Laura had ordered a second drink, and we had shared some chips and guac. When the check came, I put my credit card down and peered over the table, waiting for her to reciprocate. When she didn't, I asked her plainly if she intended to see me again for a second date.

While she was caught off guard at first, she initially responded honestly that she didn't feel like we were a good match, yada, yada, yada. You know, the generic "I'm-not-interested" line. I said that I agreed, and while I thought she was a nice person, I also didn't think that we had the same vibe.

I then asked her if she would mind putting down her credit card to split the date. It was then that she became incredulous. "Hold on," she said. "Are you telling me that you're only willing to pay the check if I was interested in a second date?"

Obviously, I confirmed her revelation. She was genuinely shocked by my boldness, and she huffed and tossed her credit card down without saying another word. To say that I was delighted would be an understatement. I felt so empowered in that moment, knowing that the old me would have never dared. *No more bullshit*, I remember thinking to myself.

Fortunately, my luck turned. In early November, I hit three solid matches on Bumble all within twenty-four hours of each other. First, there was Alex, who was a very fetching yoga instructor in the Upper East Side. Then there was Stephanie, a pediatric gastroenterologist from Canada who had just moved to start her second fellowship. And finally, there was Nancy.

Nancy was the cute blond German girl who opened up the chat on Bumble by asking me for a list of my favorite brunch places. Given that she had just moved to New York in the summer, she was looking for a new spot. I gladly obliged with a few of my favorites.

Days went by, and Nancy did not respond. In the meantime, I had my first date with Alex, and things actually went very well up until the good night kiss. Alex had been 100% tuned in for the whole evening but didn't seem too interested in the kiss at the end. There was a clear signal for possible friend vibes.

Stephanie was working a lot as a physician-in-training, so we were having trouble finding time to schedule a first date. It's always a good idea to have a few irons in the fire at once when dating in New York, so seeing as a I needed a second iron, I reached back out to Nancy on the app.

I must point out that I rarely do this, as when people ignore my messages online, I almost immediately just move on. But Nancy had cute pics, and she seemed adventurous and liked to travel, so I decided to tug the line one more time before giving up. Fortunately, she responded this time, and we quickly bantered for a bit before exchanging numbers to plan a date.

Unfortunately, this time, it was my turn to throw a wrench on things. For while I'm usually a very detail-oriented person, I actually transposed two of the digits for her phone number incorrectly into my phone. So my initial text message to "Nancy" was likely not received by someone named Nancy.

A day went by, and I hadn't heard anything back, which I thought was typical for her based on our interaction online. And I was about to give up a second time. I'm not sure exactly why I thought to go back into Bumble and check the number again, but when I did, I immediately noticed my mistake. Hastily, I reentered the number and resent the text.

Again, hours went by. Given that I had fucked it up the first time, I went back and checked the paper where I had written down her number, only to discover that I had transcribed it incorrectly *a second time* into my phone.

"Mother of Christ!" I shouted aloud as the cat slept onward, ignoring my late-evening buffoonery. I finally tried again, and after three times, I successfully reached Nancy.

I did explain to her what had happened with the mistake (I only told her it happened once), and she was actually quite amused. She replied back that it would be fun if the other person showed up, and that perhaps if they did, we could have a threesome. "Hmph," I chuckled to myself. "This girl seems very funny."

Upon finally meeting Nancy, she was, in fact, very funny. We met at the Bar Veloce on the corner of my street in Hell's Kitchen, where she told me that she was sadly not able to drink because she was afflicted with some rare form of long COVID-19, whereby even a single drink would produce a profound hangover the following day.

We made a joke of it, poking fun at her being a cheap date—that is, until I told her that I texted two others before finally getting her number right, at which she made the remark that the date would be quite expensive if all the invited parties would eventually show up. After enjoying a round of drinks and swapping basic life details, we moved next door to enjoy some authentic Thai food at this local spot that I love on Ninth Avenue named Der Krung.

I know what you're thinking right now. This old fool is going back to the well of Thai-food-induced disaster on another early date. Did he not learn anything? Well, to respond to that, I'll say that the heart wants what it wants; and I love Thai food even it if doesn't love me back. Also, I was five hundred yards from my apartment this time, so I could easily sprint home this time if my weak bowels acted up again.

Our first date continued to be laced with humor at every opportunity. Der Krung was very hot that night, which is typical for most establishments in New York, who are generally unable to effectively regulate their internal temperatures in any season. At one point, I was forced to remove my sweater lest I devolve into a sweaty beast. As I sat there in a T-shirt, I could see Nancy very obviously checking me out as we nibbled on spicy Thai chicken wings.

"Have you always been so sporty?" she inquired in her adorable German accent.

I delighted that she thought my fortysomething year old ass was still sporty and chuckled to myself as I wondered if her comment was born from some European stereotype of Americans being overweight. I also hadn't heard the word sporty in about twenty years, so this was also very funny to me at the time.

After dinner, I walked her home, and we shared our first kiss like most New Yorkers do: on the street in front of someone's apartment, in full display for any of their passing neighbors to see. *Ah, what a feeling to be alive and be back on the hunt again*, I remember thinking on my way back to my apartment. The date had just ended, but I was already looking forward to seeing Nancy again soon.

Dating in New York is rarely linear, as most people are not seeing one person at a time. My path to my second date with Nancy was certainly serpentine, as I had two other irons in the fire that I needed to attend to. Next up was Alex, who came with me to my yoga studio for our second date. This seemed like a good idea, what with her being a yoga instructor and all, and the added bonus was that she would meet my friends at the studio.

While things were progressing well with Alex, I was finally able to get Stephanie out for a first date. We decided to spend a rainy, freezing winter Sunday afternoon at the Monet immersion experience downtown. I didn't quite know what to expect from this experience, but I was pleasantly surprised. In addition to many famous paintings and plaques that highlighted the artist and his various works, there was an opportunity to sit down and color. This was sublimely fun, as we were each trying to create our own lily pad, which would then be scanned into a computer and projected onto a virtual "pool" to float around with the other lily pads that the other patrons had made.

Sitting in the tiny chairs at the tiny table, which seemed obviously intended for children, Stephanie and I were able to get acquainted. We swapped stories of our journeys through the medical profession, how we each landed in New York, and what we were looking for in prospective partners. My own severe artistic limitations notwithstanding, we had a great time at the Monet exhibit.

Afterward, we danced through the puddles, which had formed nicely on the cobblestone streets of the FiDi, to a coffee shop turned cocktail bar named Split Eights. Once there, we recused ourselves from the nasty weather and sat neatly tucked away in the corner, sipping two glasses of prosecco. As it was now fairly late in the afternoon on a Sunday in the FiDi, we pretty much had the place to ourselves.

Stephanie was slender and petite, with a full mane of red hair and stone-blue eyes. She nestled quite nicely under my arm, as we swapped stories of our childhood and our siblings. Before I was even expecting it, she leaned into me slowly, and we shared our first kiss, tucked away together in a tiny dimly lit cocoon, somehow ensconced in our own little world while being surrounded by some of the busiest buildings in all the free world.

Before the evening carried on for very long, the barista turned barkeep advised us to depart for closing time. Reluctantly, we shed our indoor skin, and donned the layers of clothes and rain gear required to get back to the subway. As I dropped Stephanie off at her subway station, I pulled her in for another kiss, this one in classic romance movie fashion—guys kisses girl in the rain, unperturbed by the weather or the throngs of passersby as they attempt to elude the elements and get home in time for supper.

While the first date had gone well with Stephanie, I was steadfast in my quest and my commitment to the process. Indeed, the old me would have jumped at the positive initial experiences with any of these three women and probably abandoned the others in my anxiety-driven desire to bypass the journey as a means to an expedited end. And so enjoying my newfound freedom from anxiety, I stayed true to my heart, trusted the process, and continued seeing all three women.

Date three with Alex was a big one, as I had scored last-minute tickets to see *Fiddler on the Roof* in Yiddish. I had never seen the play, and Alex was Jewish, so I knew this would be super fun and would score me a lot of "points." To top off the evening, I made a reservation at the Grand Boucherie in Midtown. This glorious venue, with its sweeping buttressed arches and massive outdoor space that spans an entire city block, is a must-see attraction for anyone seeking old-world charm in the center of the city that has it all. The food's not half bad either.

Alex looked magnificent that night, dressed to the nines in a long, elegant white dress. The evening was a total surprise to her. She didn't even find where we were dining until an hour or so before our reservation. She was blown away, and we sat about as close as humanly possible during the entire production of *Fiddler*, our legs intertwined and our hands firmly clasped together. Alex was just a smidge shorter than I, so her head rested perfectly on my shoulder for most of the performance.

The evening went swimmingly to say the least. After the show, we walked back to my apartment to grab my car so that I could drive her home. Alex's street was completely full of parked cars, so I pulled up in front of a pile of trash near her place. Again, this is dating in New York, folks.

After making sure that I wasn't about to get attacked by a rabid raccoon from the trash heap, I opened Alex's door and took her hand to escort her home properly. The entire evening was culminating toward our kiss, which I was sure would stop the galaxies as they orbited each other in the nothingness of space. And then with all the sexual tension and romance of a magical evening packed into one moment, I suffered through one of the most awkward make out sessions of my entire life.

I am aware of the nerves that accompany dating in any place, let alone New York. And certainly, after an evening like the one that Alex and I had, I can appreciate where both parties might be nervous. However, Alex was in her late thirties and I in my early forties, so neither of us were inexperienced in the game of love at this point in our lives. And unfortunately, this kiss on our third date was somewhat in line with the two prior dates, where we didn't seem to match up physically with how much we obviously liked each other personally.

At this point, driving home from this date, I was starting to doubt my connection with Alex. While I don't want to overstress the importance of the physical side of relationships, I do believe that physical compatibility is really important for couples. Long-term monogamy is very hard, and it usually requires a very strong physical connection to stand the test of time. While Alex and I clearly had compatibility in many areas, it was starting to become evident that we might lack the physical connection necessary to sustain us in the long-term.

These doubts proved critical, for if that date with Alex had ended the way I expected it to, I might not have pursued the other women. But with my head clouded with uncertainty about Alex, I kept on with my quixotic quest. Next up was a second date with Nancy.

We had arranged to meet on the corner of Fifty-Third and Ninth Avenue. On my way down to meet Nancy, I spontaneously stopped at a bodega to grab a single red rose for the date. That decision would prove to be pivotal.

I met Nancy in front of the meatball dispensary. It was cold, and we were both bundled up, but she looked smart in her form fitting black dress, which I could see buried under her black topcoat. Nancy was very attractive, standing about my height with eyes that appeared a light-blue shade, at least under the backdrop of streetlights and the inky black winter night sky. While she made a comment about my "sportiness" on our first date, she was very fit herself, and I later found out that she liked to swim after work.

She saw the rose and immediately perked up. She thought it was very sweet and threw her arms around me and hugged me very tightly. *Well, things are off to a good start*, I thought to myself.

We started the evening in a bar called Hell's Kitchen for a drink. She was still not drinking, so I enjoyed a Christmas-themed cocktail in what was unbeknownst to me a holiday-themed bar. Indeed, it had nailed to the ceiling a fully decorated Christmas tree upside down, and the entire interior was adorned in holiday decorations and lights from all faiths and religions. It was simultaneously festive and goofy, which was exactly the right atmosphere for Nancy to shine. We spent our time there laughing, mostly at the decor, but we were definitely taking playful jabs at each other.

After the bar, we went to a nice place on the corner of Forty-Fourth and Tenth Avenue (aptly named forty-four by ten) and enjoyed an intimate dinner. Nancy was a little obsessed with the rose (in a cute way), and she was taking lots of pictures of it lying on the table in between a pair of flickering candles. While it was clearly an impulse purchase, the rose had somehow turned into the star of the show.

The food was good, albeit ordinary, but something happened that night at dinner. I felt this very serene sense wash over me, and I felt utterly comfortable and at home in her presence. We weren't talking about anything in particular, just more of the usual second-date stuff. What was happening wasn't necessarily based on anything that was happening or being said, it was just occurring. I suppose this is actual definition of "vibing" with someone, and our vibe was tranquil, calm, and relaxed.

After dinner, I escorted Nancy home, and we had a longer make out session in front of her building this time. On my way home, I kept thinking about that feeling that I had at dinner and what it could have meant. I was surprised and perplexed to have connected with someone on a subconscious level so quickly like that, and I was most definitely intrigued enough by that feeling to want to see more of Nancy.

Stephanie was proving hard to pin down for dates, as she was pretty much only available on Sunday afternoons. As this was in November and the peak of football season, she was forcing me to make some tough decisions between dating and doing the things I really enjoyed. A prior version of me, one anxious and obsessed with finding the one, would have probably acquiesced to her schedule requirements and abandoned my lovable Lions for an afternoon with Stephanie. My present self, however, was not willing to make that compromise.

Alex, on the other hand, was very easy to schedule dates with; and we made plans to see each other about a week after our third date. At this point, I was a bit apprehensive about Alex. On the one hand, I really liked her. She was sweet, funny, athletic, attractive, easygoing, and funny. But this string of disastrous kisses was starting to weigh on me. I knew that I needed to escalate things if I was to get my answer about our physical compatibility. So I pulled out the dating trump card and invited her over to my place for a home-cooked dinner.

Cooking for someone is a very sweet proposition. Food is at the center of nearly every culture on earth, and taking the time and care to prepare a meal for someone is a universal kindness. As an added benefit, inviting someone over provides a nice opportunity for privacy, something that is generally lacking in the early phases of New York City dating. This, of course, only works if one doesn't have roommates, which is the main reason that I never even considered having one. Nothing kills the date vibe more than having your roommate stumble into the kitchen in his underwear and cut a loud fart while you're on the couch, making out with a date. Not cool.

I decided to go for my ace dish, roasted chicken with asparagus. It's a remarkably simple meal, but because it's a whole roasted chicken, it comes off as fancier and more sophisticated than it really is. I pulled it off without a hitch, and afterward, we were enjoying some wine on the couch when disaster struck.

Alex leaned in and started kissing my neck, which I quickly reciprocated. What happened next can only be described as a collision between two completely incompatible human beings. When I say everything was out of sync, I mean everything. Our lips were in the wrong place at the wrong time. Our hips were out of sync like two people at a silent disco dancing to different songs. Literally when I zigged, she zagged.

As a result of this complete disconnection, I actually stopped focusing on the make out and started to contemplate my exit strategy. How was I going to get out of this predicament without being a douche or doing something hurtful? I still had no intentions of hurting her feelings, and I was desperately racking my brain for a gracious escape plan.

Then I remembered all the times that my aging body had failed me and how many prior dates were derailed due to my collection of ailments. How I wished in that moment that some plague would intervene, and I could let Alex down gracefully without any shame or embarrassment.

Wishing an ailment doesn't make it happen, and as the erratic make out session continued, my body was (unfortunately) holding up just fine. So I did the only thing I could think of to do, and I faked it.

No, not an orgasm! An injury, of course. I decided that my old man back was my best bet, so I needed to create a scenario to fake an injury. So I grabbed Alex with both of my arms around her back, pulled her in close so that her legs were now wrapped around my torso, and promptly stood up. I took two steps toward my bedroom and then abruptly stopped and let out a fabricated yelp of pain.

I immediately dropped Alex onto her feet and grabbed pitifully at my back. She was surprised but immediately acted, asking what she could do to help.

I stumbled to the couch and asked for her to get me an ice pack from the fridge. She stayed awhile, offering to help in various ways, but I reassured her that this was an unfortunate part of my reality, and when my back goes out, all I can do is rest and give it time. Eventually, she showed herself out but only after telling me repeatedly how much fun she had and how she couldn't wait to see me again.

I would later let Alex down gently over the phone, and while I did feel some guilt for the lie, I did not dwell too long on the matter. I knew that I had done the right thing by following my gut and ending things early before any feelings were involved.

Stephanie was still MIA, but fortunately, I was able to schedule my third date with Nancy only a few days after my final date with Alex. This time, Nancy and I were going to the Bryant Park winter village, which is where they transformed the park into an ice-skating rink and a collection of shops purveying Christmas-themed items.

Nancy and I met along Sixth Avenue and walked down the park hand in hand. Nancy looked as lovely as ever, with her long blond hair and her hazel-green eyes, which had seemingly changed color by being paired with her green sweater. We were both wearing green sweaters, actually, a fun coincidence that we joked about multiple times during our date.

When we arrived at the park, I ordered what I thought was a normal G and T, only to be handed a home-wrecker G and T. Nancy was still abstaining and ordered a diet Dr Pepper.

After guzzling this rocket fuel, I needed food, so we found a food hut that was dispensing ready to order cacio e pepe. After consuming our piping hot pasta on an ice-cold park bench, we opted for a transition to warmer temperatures. Nancy suggested that we hit the rooftop at the Peninsula Hotel.

We arrived and were seated promptly, which surprised me given how posh this rooftop bar was. Nancy and I sat closely together and continued the beautiful process of getting to know someone potentially special. Unfortunately, despite the two bowls of hummus and pita that we consumed, I was getting quite drunk from the strong drinks the hotel was serving. I don't remember much from our time at the Peninsula, but at one point, I was so enamored with the fact that we were both wearing green sweaters that I stuck my hand into her sleeve. On the inside, Nancy was laughing hysterically at this move (or so she tells me), but at the moment, we were still sitting center stage in the middle of a very swanky bar, so she gently removed my hand from her sleeve and carried on with the evening.

After we left the Peninsula, I walked her home, and we had another longer kiss on the street. I was drunk enough to push the issue, and I invited myself up to her place for another drink. Politely and appropriately, she declined my self-invitation, telling me that she was not prepared for a visitor that night. We finished our make out sesh, and I stumbled drunkenly home, feeling very full, both literally and figuratively.

Nancy and I, despite our initial dating successes, were facing a dire obstacle. For you see, dear reader, Nancy had booked at two-and-a-half-week trip home to Germany; and she was set to leave on

December 15. As for our fourth date, that left us with little time to see each other before she would leave for what is considered an eternity in the world of modern dating.

Fortunately, Nancy and I were both determined to see what we had going, so we booked our fourth date soon after our third. Given that I felt that we also needed some privacy to get to know each other, I invited her over to my apartment for dinner. I was also just really excited to cook for her, as I'd really enjoyed my time with her up to that point. Rather than my traditional safe dish of roasted chicken, I decided to be more bold with Nancy. I selected a newly discovered recipe for a pretzel-crusted pork chop with roasted brussels sprouts. My hope was that the pretzel-coated meat would speak to her German heritage and also convey to her how much I liked her already.

My menu choice must have worked because Nancy and I slept together that night. Nancy and I were in total sync with each other, mentally, physically, and emotionally. The evening was perfect, even better than I could have hoped for.

Distance be damned, I remember thinking to myself as I drifted off to sleep. I knew that Nancy was absolutely worth waiting for.

Epilogue

Well, dear reader, if you haven't figured it out yet, I was the snoring boar that jolted poor, sweet Nancy from her peaceful slumber on the eve of our fourth date. A consequence of aging and perhaps my expanding waistline, I had recently picked up that nasty little habit upon entering my fifth decade of life. When you add the snoring to the allergies, the insomnia, the old man back, and the weak bowels, you've got the total package, really. It's no surprise that Nancy was powerless to resist my geriatric charms.

In all seriousness, finding Nancy was a blessing. Despite her long absence to Germany, we kept in close touch over the Christmas holidays. Since she returned to New York in the New Year, we've been almost inseparable.

Dating Nancy has been so easy because we match up in so many ways: our energy level, our activities, our commitment to our health, our commitment to social justice, our incredibly strange senses of humor, and our love of animals. She has earned the cat's approval, which would have been a deal-breaker otherwise. Most importantly, Nancy and I are committed to ourselves first and foremost. We take care of our mental health, and in doing so, we become stronger partners to each other. We've also established excellent lines of communication, so whenever there have been disagreements or misunderstandings, we have been able to quickly talk through them and support each other emotionally.

Since we started dating, my back has blown out (for real this time). And Nancy was there every step of the way taking care of me. One of my dear friends was getting married when this happened, and Nancy helped me get dressed for the ceremony and held me up on the dance floor so that no one around us knew how bad off I was.

Later, Nancy tripped on some uneven pavement and broke both elbows. She actually did; I'm not making that up, both elbows! Honestly, when that happened, I knew that I had found my geriatric counterpart; or someone who was at least as disaster prone as I was. While I was really sad that happened and felt bad for Nancy, as she missed an important work trip out West, I was a little bit relieved to have the opportunity to reciprocate and take care of her for once.

Finding Nancy and winning her heart so soon after conquering my own demons cannot be coincidence. I strongly suspect that if I hadn't gotten my shit together, Nancy would not have picked me. Or if she did, I would have likely fucked it up with my neediness and my anxious attachment style.

However, after falling for Nancy, my feelings about my past began to change. I stopped beating myself up for waiting so long to take care of my mental health because I was suddenly grateful that it had prevented me from ending up with any of the other girls I had dated in New York. I started seeing the mental illness itself as a means to an end, as it kept me from ending up (again) with someone who wasn't the right person for me. It was painful to suffer through those years, consumed by anxiety and dread. But in the end, it led me to Nancy.

Much like the muse of this book, Don Quixote, I found myself strengthened greatly by my setbacks and suffering. On his deathbed, Don Quixote calls out, "Blessed be the Almighty God who has done so much for me! His mercies are limitless." This he felt, despite all the failures that had beset him in his travels. Don Quixote's belief in his quest and in himself absolutely resonates with me as I sit here today, telling my own tail of failure, setback, and suffering.

However, unlike Don Quixote, who returned home to die in his bed, I have ended my quest victorious. I am triumphant over my own past and my demons. I have found myself, and in seeking love, I have learned the true meaning of it. And in finding Nancy, I have found that "feeling" that has always eluded me. I feel certain that, at age forty-two, I have finally discovered that feeling of unbridled joy that comes with finding one's forever person.

Nancy grew up in Germany behind an actual wall made of stone and wire. And she was only able to pursue her dreams, learn English, and move abroad after the wall came down. I also grew up behind a wall, but mine was invisible, and it was constructed out of an absence of self-trust and self-worth. Like Nancy, I was only able to achieve my dream of finding true love after my own wall came down.

It's funny to think how a girl from East Germany and a boy from Michigan managed to find each other amid the chaos that is now post-pandemic New York. But through the wonders of online dating apps and through a lot of luck, that's exactly what we did.

And that, dear reader, is my happy ending. Or perhaps more accurately, my happy beginning.

CHAPTER 10

Closing Thoughts and Words of Wisdom

Blessed be the Almighty God who has done so much
for me! His mercies are limitless, and they're not
reduced or restrained by the sins of men.

—Don Quixote de la Mancha

Thank you, dear reader, for sticking with me to this point. I promise that, like the great Don Quixote himself, I am nearly finished.

In this book, we followed the journey of a Bumble-ing, un-Hinged semi-old man as he quested through New York during a global pandemic in search of true love. Along the way, he battled numerous physical ailments, including broken bones, swollen eyes, and a failing back. Oh, and he nearly shat himself. Truly, the parallels between this modern-day aged hero and the venerable Don Quixote of yesteryear, who also slogged onward in his quest despite his obvious physical limitations, are plentiful.

So how did I do it? Well, here's where I get to share my tips of the trade to any single, middle-aged readers who are likewise still looking for love after thirty-five.

I know I've already mentioned this first tip, but it bears repeating. "To thine own self be true." This sounds cliché, I know, but I think it bears stating because people in their thirties and forties are people who have a dating history. Whether this is a prior divorce, children from with former spouse, or just a series of really toxic twentysomething relationships, middle-aged daters all have scars.

So my first words of advice on this particular topic are to be up front with your dates. This does a couple of things. One, if you're dating someone who is also middle-aged, this will likely create a commonality that you two can bond over, as this person will also probably have their own battle scars. By sharing yours, you can diminish their apprehension about their past and open the door for them to reciprocate, which will in the end create a very nice opportunity for you both to showcase your empathy early in the dating process.

Two, if you're not dating another middle-aged person (i.e., perhaps someone considerably younger), showing your truth up front can set the tone for the rest of the relationship. People in their twenties who have not gone through divorce or who don't have kids may not be comfortable with those situations, so it's better to be fully transparent up front rather than wasting anyone's time.

I actually experienced this quite a bit. Since I was married in a Catholic church, I cannot ever do so again, so that was a deal-breaker for anyone who really wanted a Catholic wedding. After a few encounters like that, I stopped waiting to tell my dates about my past. There's no magic number of dates to divulge these details. I would say that first date is generally too soon, so I would usually aim for spilling the beans by the third date depending on how things were going. Waiting longer than the third date feels a bit disingenuous to me.

The second part of "to thine own self be true" is to stop hiding from yourself. By the time we enter our middle-ages, we likely have scars. Sharing them with potential partners is one thing, but more importantly, we need to deal with them ourselves and be at peace with them in the first place before we even approach potential partners. After reading this book, you know that this is something that I didn't do. Indeed, I kept taking the easy way out, ignoring the past (and how I felt about it), and plunging ever forward toward the future, all the while hoping that what I would find in the future would magically fix the problems in the past that I was running from.

Sadly, as I learned, it doesn't work that way. So if you feel that in your heart that you have things to work on, or that you want to talk to someone about it, then do it. I got lucky because ignoring my mental illness actually delayed my dating plans enough for me to finally find the person that I was meant to find. But you may not be so lucky. Truly, I was very lucky because the people that I was meeting and dating were not malevolent, and none of them took advantage of me in my vulnerable emotional state. I could have just as unluckily ended up with someone with a narcissistic personality disorder or just a run-of-the-mill opportunistic gaslighter, who would have turned my already bad situation into a living hell.

So face your shit and fix it. Even if you think your shit is already fixed, do an emotional inventory and consider regular check-ins with a therapist or qualified mental health providers as you continue to live your best single life. When you do finally meet your person, you'll be so happy you did. I know that I sure am.

While the therapist will handle the important clinical stuff, there are some things that you can do to help improve your mental health from a dating perspective. Again, I am not a therapist or a licensed mental health provider. I'm just a semi-old man who likes to read, and I spent a lot of time educating myself on how to be a better partner through self-growth. So for those readers interested, here is a suggested approach to this process, using the books that I read as a foundation. If this topic doesn't interest you, feel free to skip ahead to the next topic.

For starters, all serious relationships depend on effective communication. The main problem is that for many of us, we're not even equipped with the right words to express our feelings appropriately. For that reason, I strongly recommend Brené Brown's *Atlas of the Heart*. This book is an anthology of human emotions, all of them, with painstaking research and detail. By reading this book, you will finally be armed with the language of emotions, and you will not only gain a much deeper understanding of your own feelings but you'll also be much more adept at expressing them effectively to others.

Next on the reading list is *Irritating the Ones You Love* by Jeff Auerbach. This quick little read packs a big punch, as the author posits a theory about how we are subconsciously attracted to the same people over and over again in relationships and where the origin of these patterns stems from. It's honestly a fascinating read that may change your entire perspective on dating. And if you're in therapy, this book will definitely give you ample material for your next session.

Third, I would suggest a book on attachment theory. Anyone will do honestly as long it goes into some detail about the premise. I'm not so sure that attachment theory is important in helping to find "the one" as much as it's useful in avoiding the people that we should absolutely not be with. If I say words like "anxious attachment" or "avoidant attachment" and they don't mean anything to you, then please spend some time reading up. You'll thank me when you do, especially if you discover that you have an anxious attachment style and all your exes are avoidants.

Lastly, I have to recommend the masterpiece by Prophet Ansari, *Modern Romance*. This one comes at the end of your psychological journey because it is absolutely not a modern psychology book. Rather, the author offers a variety of tips on how to survive modern dating, all with a very humorous slant. He also spends quite a bit of time giving advice on how to fix a dating profile, which is a perfect segue into my next topic.

So now that you've addressed your past, and you're comfortable with sharing it with your prospective dates, my next piece of advice involves your marketing, which if you're a contemporary dater means your online dating profile.

I had literally no help with this when I first started back in 2016. I put together what I thought would be appealing to the masses and just posted it. It took me years to finally refine my profile toward something even remotely appealing.

Step one, know your audience. Are you on Tinder or Grindr? If the answer is yes, then you're going for a casual vibe. Fun and flirtatious text along with funny pictures (likely with limited clothing) is probably your jam.

If you're a middle-aged dater like I was, you're probably not on Tinder or Grindr. And yes, there are exclusive apps like The League, which cater to a more specific audience, but I've always had the most success on Bumble and Hinge. I've had two serious relationships that came from Hinge, and I found one (likely going on two) wife come from Bumble. So at least in my personal experience, these two apps have paid the best dividends of any that I've tried.

So now that you're on the "right" platform, try to build the best profile. *Modern Romance* does a very good job providing very thorough advice on this topic, so if you want something more comprehensive, then I would read this book for sure. Here is my quick and dirty version.

Full disclaimer to you, my dear reader, that these are the ramblings of an aging brain from a cis white straight male dater. They absolutely do not reflect the broad scope of preferences from individuals who identify in any other group of daters. So with that in mind, here are my tips for your pictures:

- Showcase your face and, preferably, your eyes. We connect so much based on eye contact, so please limit sunglasses to one picture. That means no hats either, at least not in every picture.
- Showcase your whole body. I have seen far too many profiles where every picture is neck up only. Please don't do this. You're just setting yourself up for a disappointing first date if you don't let the other person see what the whole you looks like.
- Third, include one (at max two) action shots. So many profiles that I've perused over the years were all action shots. While these are fun, if you're wearing ski goggles or a makeshift turban on your desert safari in every photo, and I can't even see what you look like, then I'm going to have to pass every time, even if you seem sporty, well-traveled, and cool.
- Speaking of travel and similar to point three, try to keep these photos to a minimum of one to two pictures. For those unfamiliar with the apps, you should know that there

is generally a limit of photos, usually around six to eight. So if you're only allowed six photos, I would say two travel pictures is more than adequate. Anything more seemed a little pretentious to me. And in case anyone needs to hear this, try to be socially conscious with your pictures (i.e., no sedated tigers, please).

- Lastly, take the opportunity to be honest about yourself. If you don't want kids, put it in the profile. Don't eat meat? Put that in the profile. If the only time you dance is with the devil in the pale moonlight, then put that shit front and center. If you love hip-hop and have a diverse playlist, then share some of your favorite hits. Or better yet, connect your Spotify with your profile (Bumble does this), so I can see what you like. These things not only showcase who you are and give others an opportunity to see your true self, they provide a great icebreaker to start the first date conversation.

And my last piece of advice after you've done all that? Have fucking fun. Dating is supposed to be fun, but I think it's very common for people as they advanced into their thirties and forties to feel this enormous pressure to date with a purpose. Doing so only makes the whole process feel like work, and I've definitely been out on dates where I felt like I was on a job interview.

Don Quixote was a story about how one must live life in a passionate, genuine way no matter what other people think. I think that is the perfect mantra for middle-aged dating today. It starts with figuring out who you are, dealing with your past, and then showcasing yourself openly and unabashedly to your potential partners.

It's easy to feel self-conscious or to feel like you've lost a step compared to your younger self. Don't. Not even for a minute. You're so much more experienced than you were in your twenties, and if you embrace that mentality and tap into your inner truth and your inner strength, then you'll be unstoppable. After all, I survived two divorces, a miscarriage, a global pandemic, and countless physical ailments along my journey toward true love. And now that I have it,

I wouldn't trade it for anything in the world. For me, the journey was just as valuable as the outcome.

And so with that, dear reader, we're done. Thank you for coming on this quixotic quest with me. And for those middle-aged daters who are still out searching, I wish you Godspeed. It may be a bumpy (and at times perilous) journey, but if you stick to it, I'm confident that you'll find your own version of true love.

ABOUT THE AUTHOR

Douglas Jennings is a professor of pharmacy and has been a pharmacist for over fifteen years. As a clinician-scientist, Professor Jennings has published over one hundred manuscripts in the field of solid organ transplant. *Finding Love at Forty* is his debut book. He currently resides in New York City with a quasi-feral cat named Akira.